Antiquing with George Michael

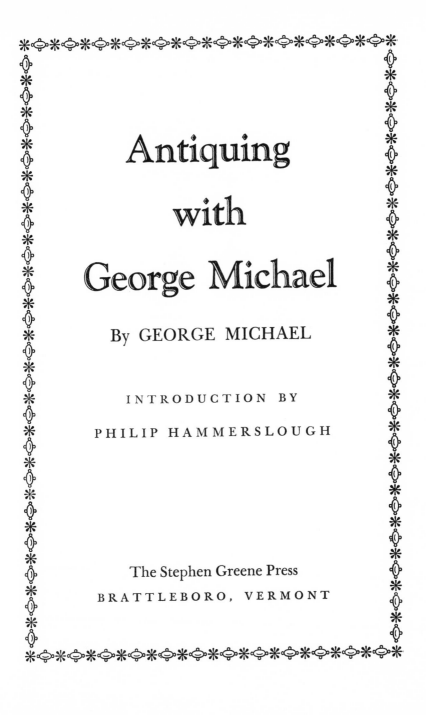

Antiquing
with
George Michael

By GEORGE MICHAEL

INTRODUCTION BY

PHILIP HAMMERSLOUGH

The Stephen Greene Press

BRATTLEBORO, VERMONT

DEDICATED TO THE MEMORY
OF FRANK ROWE, A MAN WHO
LIVED BY THE GOLDEN RULE

ACKNOWLEDGMENTS

For their kind permission to use the photographs on the pages indicated, the author is grateful to the Carnegie Institute Museum, Pittsburgh (bottom 41); *The Boston Globe* (44); WENH-TV, Durham, N. H. (45, bottom 97, 99, 100, 101 and 103); Philip Hammerslough, Esq., and Meyers Studios of Hartford (46); Richard Carter Barret, Esq., and Lloyd Studios of Bennington, Vt. (47); and the Shelburne Museum, Inc., staff photographer Einars J. Mengis (102 and 104).

Printed in the United States of America
by Vermont Printing Company.

Library of Congress catalog card number: 67-29639

Contents

CONTENTS

Introduction

To be asked by such a renowned authority on antiques as George Michael to provide some introductory comments for his book is, as the late cartoonist William Webster would have said, "the thrill that comes once in a lifetime."

Mr. Michael, with his long experience as an auctioneer, and his years in television, discussing almost every subject in the field on his nationwide weekly program *Antiques,* has written a book which performs a valuable service for both the beginner and the advanced collector alike. Forgoing the natural temptation to write a handbook or guide—which certainly, with his expertise, he would be capable of doing—he has produced instead a warm, sympathetic, and informative account of what he calls "antiquing" in America today.

There is nothing rigid about his stated preferences, other than an insistence on the qualities of integrity and taste which make an object timeless in its appeal. He discusses fads, notes changing values, offers areas for new exploration and collecting. His recommendations for searching out the treasures of regional heritages will, I am sure, have a pronounced effect, and do much to encourage local historians and collectors. He proffers tips on identification; refinishing and repairing; bidding at auctions and buying from dealers. He has an interesting chapter on his travels outside the United States, gathering background information and seeing at firsthand the places and repositories of some of the most beautiful and thrilling objects in Europe and the Americas. One of his most important sections, to me, is his discussion of "what makes an antique" in his chapter on the *why*'s and *how*'s of collecting.

Throughout his book he presents his individual philosophy in approaching antiques, stressing the importance of personal association and appreciation for the intangible values that surround carefully made, and loved, objects from our past. His anecdotes, while filled with humor and human interest, are always pertinent to his text.

In order to get a true picture of the interest which the American people have taken in antiques, I feel that it is necessary to go back to the 1920's. Up to about 1929 only the wealthy few in this country were serious collectors, but shortly thereafter there began an increasing awareness by the general public of the pleasures that could be derived from coming in contact with good American antiques; and after World War II many thousands of "everyday" people started buying antiques with which to furnish their homes.

As a result, the laws of supply and demand have had their effect, and in the past ten years the prices of good American furniture, paintings, silver, pewter, glass, pottery, and other artifacts, have risen to almost unbelievable heights. With such current prices, much of Mr. Michael's information may prove highly profitable to the prospective buyer in many ways.

I have watched practically every one of his *Antiques* programs on Educational Television, and have gained a tremendous amount of knowledge about a great many different subjects in the antique field. I am sure that my experience is shared by his large audience of viewers, and will be by the readers of this book.

July 1967   PHILIP HAMMERSLOUGH
West Hartford, Connecticut

1

The

Hall of

Decorative Arts

I T WAS a cold March day in 1964. The Hall of Decorative Arts at the Carnegie Institute in Pittsburgh was aglow, filled with tables and counters of fine and rare glassware, silver, china, brass, clocks, jewelry, oils, furniture, and all the items which one dreams of as perfect complements to his home. These were not there just for museum display, but rather to be sold at the first auction sponsored by the Women's Committee as a fund-raising project for the museum. Huge marble figures looked down from the surrounding balcony as silent witnesses to the proceedings below. The wall cases—filled with permanent displays of early Chinese pottery and carvings, Art Nouveau glass, and bronzes from early Egypt—lent additional elegance to the already colorful and intriguing displays.

I had arrived in Pittsburgh two days earlier, to help make preparations for the actual conduct of the auction and to do the sale for the committee. Meeting with the ladies of the committee was a mutual evaluation, and one which I feel has developed since into warm friendship and respect. While eating

1

lunch within an hour of our meeting, I was asked many questions on how I wanted things arranged, plus being offered many suggestions on how it should be done. Sensing that there were several diverging opinions, I remarked that I would tell them in due time what should be done. This kept our conversations at an even pace until I was asked directly why I wouldn't tell them then anything of my plans. I thanked them all for their confidence in having me come there and reminded them that all decisions must be left to me, to be made in my own good time. Also, I told them that, in my experience, letting a group of women know too far in advance what I wanted done generally gave them only more time to think up reasons why it shouldn't be done that way. This broke the ice, and I have never enjoyed the company of a group of women any more than right then as we finished lunch.

One matter that we did settle, however, was whether the auction would be stopped for a noontime recess. I suggested that this not be done. There were four hundred and forty items to dispose of, but I felt that if we started at 10:00 A.M. we should be done at 5:00 P.M. Concerning the seven-hour stint without a lunch break for me, I asked that around 12:30 I be furnished with a glass of bourbon and water from which I would sip throughout the afternoon. On the morning of the auction I was shown bourbon bottles in the handbags of no less than four of my new friends, who wanted to be sure I was well taken care of.

Meeting more of the people of Pittsburgh and its surrounding area continued to be a great experience. The day before the sale I checked the items with the inventory and went over the details of each, so as not to have to spend time doing so during the auction. Throughout these preliminaries many people sought my advice about the quality of the pieces as well as the value; and, as I have learned to expect in my occupation of handling objects that have human-interest associations, I also heard descriptions of homes and family relationships that, alone, would be enough to fill a book. These situations included wives who didn't want to reveal to their husbands how much they would be spending at the auction; mothers who planned to buy some of the finer glass, china or silver to be used as wedding presents or as gifts to their children; and newlyweds who must have budgeted their "egg money" months ahead of time in hopes of owning something that formerly graced one of Pittsburgh's fine homes.

Among my pre-auction visitors, too, were collectors who would find new pieces to add to their collections; dealers who merely expected to make a profit; students who were preparing to do papers on historical artifacts; plus fans of *Antiques* on television, who simply wanted to talk about what they owned or aspired to own some day.

A young girl of Spanish descent was completely taken with a religious painting of the early Mexican colonial period. It was at least three hundred years old, and had in one corner not only the signature of the artist but also the heads of the members of the family for whom he must have painted it. She asked how much money she should bring the next day, and I suggested the painting's worth to be around three hundred dollars. She eventually paid three hundred and ten for it, and thanked me profusely after the auction. An equally determined Spanish-looking youth had bid against her, but her confidence in my appraisal had kept her in to the end, otherwise she would have lost her courage, she told me.

Perhaps the greatest number of questions asked me, though, were by dealers who wanted more information about New England antiques, since this region is still the main source for early American objects. Books are a great help for the person who knows little about such items and wants to learn more, but often they do not delve deep enough into the fine points that interest the dealer who has long since passed his basic training. A few New England pieces, such as Connecticut clocks and glassware, had turned up for the sale—as they have continued to do in the years since. One always wonders when they came westward, and with whom.

When Governor John King of New Hampshire learned I was going down to do the 1964 auction, he asked to send along something from the people of New Hampshire as a donation to the benefit. Grace Casey of Concord was invited to make the selection, and, through the Governor's good offices, was able to get a beautiful fur cape made more than a hundred years ago in the Shaker colony in Canterbury, New Hampshire. The condition of this lovely garment was so perfect that it looked as if it had just been made; an added charm was the fact that the name of the sister who had made it was sewn inside.

The members of the organizing committee were delighted by the gift, and it was modeled by a pretty girl for a TV news spot, thus giving the sale lots of advance publicity. The Governor had sent with the cape a personal letter of documentation and best wishes to the new owner, whoever it might be. The cape went for two hundred and fifty dollars to a doctor, who said that his daughter was doing research on historical clothing, and he felt highly privileged at being able to possess it. His comment is not at all an overstatement, since it is very difficult to come by Shaker items because the Shakers are reluctant to part with them.

Most of the donations to the auction were of European origin. Pittsburgh's great importance to world commerce is seldom fully recognized by the general public, yet it is the home of many internationally known concerns like Westinghouse, Gulf, Heinz, United States Steel and similar companies, and of such notable families as the Carnegies and the Mellons. The executives in this area of concentrated wealth traveled extensively and returned home with treasures gathered from around the globe; I think the association value of objects donated from such homes lured many buyers. Another factor in the provenance of the articles given is the large number of Scottish, German and Dutch settlers, who must have brought with them tastes and desires for more things from the Old World than from the New. I imagine that imports must have become a mainstay for the dealers who bought and sold in this area.

Each year that I return to do this auction I am struck by how very rare this type of sale is, when one considers the number of museums in existence in this country. A museum provides the most desirable and perfect setting for the disposition or acquisition of art and household treasures. I can visualize dusty archives, attics, cellars, and long-forgotten storerooms filled with gifts which the museums do not use or display for one reason or another. It makes a lot of sense to clear these areas out, sell the superfluous items, and turn the money into newer and more needed or timely displays.

Of course, some museums may say that objects have been accepted with the understanding that they can never be sold. In answer, I would suggest that all museums accept such gifts only on a basis that allows the institution to do with them whatever becomes feasible at some future date. Otherwise, more years will pass with troves of idle antiques hidden away. It would be better to sell them to someone who might give them to another museum that could use them to round out its collections, or who might at least display them for the benefit of family and friends. In addition to returning many fine and historic articles to circulation, the funds realized could do much to help defray the rising costs of adequate maintenance alone.

Around the edges of preparing for the auction we took time to sightsee and explore. We found the displays in the museum fascinating, but no less so is the city itself. From Mount Washington we had a commanding view of Pittsburgh and the confluence of the Allegheny and Monongahela rivers, which forms the Ohio. Our good friend Charles Geswaldo introduced

5

us to several fine restaurants, took us on tours of the restored areas of the city, and was very helpful in getting us to the Museum of the Historical Society of Western Pennsylvania. These excursions, and the basically European look of the city, with the architecture varying from one section to another, made it much more interesting to do this auction, and I eagerly awaited the challenge.

It was not long in coming. People were waiting at the gates at nine o'clock, although the sale was not scheduled to start until ten. The Hall soon filled to capacity with dealers and collectors from miles around—some from Ohio, Kentucky and New York State—with more viewers from Chicago, and several from New York City. Outstanding among the donated items were a pair of Doughty birds, the small glass-housed figures handmade by Dorothy Doughty in England, some of which at present command prices in five figures. There was furniture, mostly English mahogany; fine oriental rugs, much elegant European glass, china and silver, and choice items of glass and pottery native to the western Pennsylvania area. As the auction got under way I sensed a camaraderie with the people gathered in the Hall, all of whom seemed to know me from my television program. This rapport with the audience is important to an auctioneer. I have had fellow auctioneers refuse to stand up to sell in front of a group of strangers in an area where they are not known. As one colleague put it: "You don't have anyone to pick on; nobody to call by name; nobody to joke with."

I must admit, an auctioneer can do a much better job when he knows which buyers are interested in particular antiques. He is inclined to watch these bidders more carefully, and encourage them to go higher, especially when he might have sold a similar item to them recently for a higher price. He also saves time that would otherwise be spent working on a bidder who may have no interest other than recognizing a good buy so long as it is cheap enough. And no matter how important the occasion or the merchandise, I agree that a certain amount of levity is enjoyed by any audience, provided it is in good taste and does not delay the proceedings. The Pittsburgh group was no exception, as has been borne out by my being invited back each year since then to perform the same task.

One of the pleasures in returning is that Pittsburgh is rich in history and dynamic in culture. I don't think the schoolbooks have ever done this city justice. Unlike such storied places as Boston, Portsmouth, New Bedford or Newburyport in my home region, Pittsburgh has not been credited with its rightful measure of cultural achievement. The result, however, is that Pittsburgh has a greater impact on the visitor because he does not expect to see what he sees.

As a student of Americana I of course knew that its reputation for glass-making predates that of New England, for in the early 1790's its glass was being shipped downriver to as far away as New Orleans; its blue-gray stoneware is prized by collectors, and the works of its old-time craftsmen in many fields are turning up more and more. Yet it is only comparatively recently that the great expansion of the erstwhile "Smoky City" has received nationwide recognition, and the cultural facilities long enjoyed by its residents are now regarded as among the foremost in the United States. The people take pride in what is built and preserved here: their spirit epitomizes the driving force which is prompting citizens of similar areas to be concerned with the past of their own communities.

As a professional handler of antiques I think it is impossible to overestimate the contribution that such study and restoration are making to our heritage, both nationally and regionally. And these efforts produce a further benefit of creating ideal showcases from which everyone—from the newest enthusiast up to the most distinguished expert—can learn more about the engrossing subject of "antiquing."

One has but to travel the country to find much historic and

7

important material which has been brought to light, restored, and preserved by dedicated people. The awakening of interest in all forms of art, whether old or new, seems to be the product of an affluent society whose members are looking for new outlets of interest and action. Restorations are very much in vogue on a community basis, but the remarkable interest in the private restoration of homes has amazed the most zealous historians. Many old country farmhouses, as well as the more classic Georgian town houses, are being snapped up at relatively little cost, because of their size, and are being totally renovated by occupants who are interested enough to restore them to their original state. They make ideal homes for the larger families of today and provide their owners with the great satisfaction of a job well done. In colonial times, the home was the center of everything, and it is amazing how functional they were with the primitive artifacts designed for them. The more classic homes that came after the Revolutionary War in great abundance are still copied today by architects who wish authenticity in the design of new construction.

Why this concerted effort to preserve and restore? Why this continuing desire for certain styles of homes and the furniture in them? Why the great demand for artifacts of the past, and a return to living in surroundings of more than a century ago? Have artisans since then been so unproductive in design and construction as to fail to excite many of today's people with their efforts? How many people do you know who have been impressed with the grandeur of the great homes of early America, although they may not know why?

The answer to these questions could be that, even aside from historical considerations, the work of those times was done in such excellent taste and design that the results are timeless, and will remain so.

I recall the day Mary Vaughan of the *Washington Star* took me for a tour of the national capital and its environs. This included the White House, shortly after work initiated by Mrs. Eisenhower had been carried through to completion by Mrs. Kennedy. The Oval Room, which had been the subject of some controversy, was on our tour. The wallpaper had been taken from an old mansion and restored on the walls of this delightful reception room at a reported cost of $35,000; the size of this particular expenditure aroused discussion as to whether it was justified. I can only admire Mrs. Kennedy for her perseverance, and believe the country can thank her for a job well done. The paper is a scenic one, going completely around the room, and aids in creating a fitting entrance for dignitaries to see. We can be proud that our White House is such a showplace: when we examine its contents, we find the craftsmanship of the past enshrined there, with nothing in the public rooms from the present except a few oils.

When we went on to Mount Vernon, Mary wanted to know my first impression as I entered. I asked her to promise not to print it in the interview, but told her that any auctioneer is overwhelmed by such an abundance of early treasures—especially those owned by such a famous man—and instinctively my first thought was, "What a wonderful place for an auction!" George Washington is my favorite man of all times in this country. The problems he faced during the Revolution and his Presidency seem to me to make many of our present-day problems pale in comparison. I was allowed in his bedroom to examine his books and other personal effects, and I couldn't help but be moved by the feeling that this great man was still very much there in spirit. At the time, a member of the staff said that they had received a nightgown supposedly belonging to him, and indeed might be the one he wore at the time he passed away, and remarked that documenting the facts could take some time. I mention this to show the importance of any article that is likely to have belonged to someone so famous.

Still another facet of antiques in America was revealed at

our next stop, the home of Mr. and Mrs. Herbert May. Here we were given a private viewing of an almost breath-taking collection of European and Russian antiques, the latter unmatched by any I have seen in traveling around western Europe. We in the United States are exposed to so little Russian art—yet here were numerous items not possessed in our best museums, or even in notable museums abroad. Marvin Ross, the curator, was very kind in offering information relative to such articles. At the time, I realized anew that art abounds in many different and wonderful forms. The work of Russian craftsmen, as well as that of artisans imported from France and Italy, especially, to create objects for the Czars, was blended into the most tasteful combination of antiques into a warm, comfortable setting, that I have ever seen in any classic home.

Later on I shall offer my views on what constitutes a collectible antique available in America. Meanwhile I hope I have shown that ethnic backgrounds are usually the determining factors in taste. In this country we find areas settled by people of differing national origins who have filled their homes with items from their native lands. The influence of these foreign crafts is felt in the native pieces made by later generations, and creates much interest in their design.

But some of us do not have one specific cultural heritage, so we learn to like what appeals to us. My father came to this country from near Balbeek, Syria, which is reputed to be the oldest city in the world—older even than Damascus. The New York Fair of 1964 had an interesting display of the art and culture of this community. I recall my father's telling us that the history of Syria was the most important subject to study in school, for the alphabet which we use today originated in Balbeek; and the world's first sailors, who came from Syria, invented nautical instruments still very much usable today—in fact, they had been improved on only slightly until the advent of the electronic age.

End of an Odyssey

My father was only twelve years old when he arrived at Boston on a cattle boat, accompanied by an elder brother and with just eight dollars in his pocket. He supported himself in Boston until he was eighteen, then took to the road with a pack on his back filled with needles, pins, thread, and other assorted merchandise to peddle from farm to farm. He and his brother would walk north from Boston to the Canadian border, and return by a different route. They lodged with families on the way, learning fluent French as well as English because they met so many French-Canadian families in their travels. Little did he know that many years later I would be calling on many of these same people to buy antiques! He learned to love New Hampshire, and determined that when he married he would settle down in Rochester, his favorite town.

My mother was born in Lebanon, the land of the fabulous olive groves, and great cedars that built Solomon's temple. When she was very young, she and her sister were brought to this country as wards of the Williams family of Springfield, Massachusetts, who owned a beautiful estate called Round Hill, located at that time just on the edge of the city. The Williamses had met my mother's people in Lebanon on one of their frequent trips around the world, and begged to take the girls home with them to raise in the States. At Round Hill they had a very happy upbringing in a background reflecting many different cultures. The home, which I saw many years later, was filled with antique objects from virtually every land. I remember particularly the oriental rugs that defied adequate description, and tall, paper-thin Satsuma vases that reached from floor to ceiling, each a work of art.

When my father settled in Rochester, he invested in real estate and bought much Main Street property. Included in one parcel, right in the middle of town, was a house built in 1752. He felt a sentimental attachment for it, because it was there that, as a boy, he had spent his first night in Rochester. From being a boarding house it was subsequently changed

11

slightly to house various businesses; and as time went by, people would remark to my father that it should be torn down, as it was such an old structure. Even after my father passed away in 1956, they made these same comments to my family. We would never touch it, though, because we knew Pop had a great fondness for it, and so far as we were concerned it would stand for as long as we owned it.

When it burned from unknown causes a few years ago and the remains had to be torn down, it was the end of an old building to many people in the community, but to my family and me it was the end of an era. This man who had come from a far-off land had left nine children with a feeling for the past and an education with which to meet the future. Now his favorite building was gone, but the little upstairs room in which he had spent his first night in the community would always exist in our memories.

When I went into business, I asked my father what he considered the best form of advertising.

His answer was: "Gossip. Just get the people talking kindly about you, and you'll always be a success, because they will advertise you."

He also reminded me that "You always make your money when you buy, not when you sell; goods well bought are half sold."

I think of him and his advice whenever I go out to buy, and I thought of him as I looked out over the crowd in the Hall of Decorative Arts at the Carnegie Institute and I started the auction in March 1964. This country is truly the land of opportunity. The fact of someone from a very small town in New Hampshire being able suddenly to make friends via television across the nation, is the kind of Horatio Alger story that is being enacted every day. I feel that so long as one works diligently every day, and does not expect life to owe him a living, he can make a success of anything.

2

From
Radio to
Barn No. 3

U<small>NCLE</small> F<small>RANK</small> R<small>OWE</small> and I had just left the doorway of an old farmhouse near Gilmanton Iron Works, New Hampshire, the reputed locale of *Peyton Place*. It had been a routine call to look at antiques, with the man of the household asking seven hundred dollars for a tall clock worth about three hundred at the time, and wanting other inflated prices for a few assorted goodies he had.

"What do you think of that for a wild goose chase?" I remarked as we got into the car.

He snorted. "I learned today never to try to do business with a man who wears short pants and sandals."

I pondered that one as we drove away, for the values Frank Rowe placed on people and things were definable by him only in pithy terms that reflected his knowledge of the ways of the world and his personal adherence to the Golden Rule: Do unto others as you would have them do unto you. I had been acquainted with "Uncle Frank" and his family since my childhood in Rochester, but at the time of our visit to Gilmanton

Iron Works in early February of 1951 what had been a casual relationship was beginning to grow into deep friendship. His attitude toward everybody was one of complete honesty, and he resented pomposity, class distinction, and ignorance. This was the man who would travel with me for ten more years through the countryside of New Hampshire and Maine, visiting people from all walks of life in search of the elusive sleepers in antiques.

At the end of November 1950 I had started the first of my still-running consignment auctions in my hometown near the Maine border. Leaving a career in radio and television in Albany, New York, to embark on such a project was rather a challenge at the time. After my studies at Emerson College and war service had come two years with WGY in Schenectady, and their pioneering television station, WRGB. By 1950 my wife, Bette, and I had small twin sons, and had been doing quite well with a husband-and-wife radio program on WROW-fm in the Capital District, with sponsors, guests every day, exciting trips with a tape recorder to conventions in upstate areas. We had a microphone on the kitchen table of our home in Rensselaer, just across the Hudson River from Albany, and we played host to many celebrities for three years.

But perhaps the work I did in farm programing for the station at the time had the greatest influence on my career, for this is what got me into the auction business, and changed our lives completely.

Near by there were two outstanding livestock auctions, one in Amsterdam and one in Waterford, which attracted buyers from several hundred miles. These were run by Carl and Fred Graziane, two of the nicest people anyone could meet. By chance, I attended one of Freddie's auctions in Waterford and recorded the auctioneer in action, playing the tape on several mornings as part of a farm program to show the prices being received on the open market at that time. It proved so popular with the farm people that the brothers bought time on the station, and my trips to the auctions became a regular weekly event.

These sales would start at 2 P.M. and end at about 11 P.M. During this time about three or four hundred calves, two to three hundred cows, and upwards of a hundred bulls would pass through the ring. These animals were mostly for butchering, so the farmers as much as two hundred miles away would listen to the prices on the radio, daily, as a guide to the worth of their stock, and it led to heavier consignments for the auctions. The "Voice of America" asked for a tape to be played around the world. I believe they wanted it to show the manner in which American farm products were sold, and how such instant on-the-spot reporting helped to create more sales and better prices.

Farmers would bring their livestock from as far away as Canada, since our radio signal went way above the border. The Canadian milch cows always commanded high prices, with these and breeding stock being sold at a more leisurely pace than the rapid-fire chant which disposed of ordinary canners and cutters. A commission on each sale was paid to the auction house.

The sessions in Waterford were especially enjoyable. After the auctions Freddie Graziane's wife would serve up to all the help a huge batch of chicken in milk gravy on dropped biscuits, with a large salad and Italian wine. Then would come out the stories about the happenings of the day. The camaraderie of these people was very different from that in my regular broadcasting work. Somehow they seemed to live under no pressures, working hard one day a week and spending the rest of the time visiting, dickering, buying, and just plain resting. To one like myself, who worked six days a week in a business filled with pressures and tensions, this system had great appeal.

Early in 1950 I was engaged by the Chatham (New York)

Area Auction Co-operative to help build interest in their auction, and it was here I witnessed the combination of selling livestock along with household goods, farm products, antiques, farm equipment, and so forth. Having come from antique country, I discussed with my wife the possibility of an auction of this type as a complete change from what we were doing. I took a leave of absence to travel to New Hampshire in search of a location where such an auction would be a novelty and could succeed. Discovering that my hometown had more cows in it than any area besides Concord, it seemed best to locate there, near a ready source of supply. So we uprooted and moved back to Rochester, and set the 30th of November as the date for my first auction.

We got off to a slow start, and it wasn't until the ninth week that careful figuring disclosed a profit: a total of sixteen cents after nearly two months of losses. We celebrated that night with dinner out.

The trouble was that the selling of livestock was considerably more difficult in New Hampshire than it was in New York. My home state had in effect the nation's first and most effective brucellosis-control program, which stipulated that no animals could be sold unless they had been inspected and certified by a veterinarian within thirty days of sale; bringing cattle in from out of state was even more complicated. Gradually, therefore, the emphasis shifted to selling household goods and other merchandise—and in turn led to my growing interest in, and search for, antiques.

Those early days in Barn No. 3 at Rochester Fairgrounds were exciting ones. We had installed bleachers and a couple of barrel stoves in one of the barns which were used to display cattle at fair time, and had a good country atmosphere as well as an authentic fragrance. People came from miles around, as this was new to them, and the consignments were very heavy. At that time people seemingly had spent their extra money earned during the war, and we had a slump in the early Fifties. The auction made it possible for them to convert things around the home into instant cash, so in it came by the truckload. Dealers sought us out for supplies for their shops from a radius of a hundred miles and into Massachusetts. Our farthest consignments came from Pennsylvania, New Jersey and Delaware. These were from campers who would haul up trailer-loads of unused goods that they could not dispose of around their home areas.

In would come farm products like corn, tomatoes, country butter, and lots of live animals and poultry. When people cleaned out attics and barns, we would get loads of barrels and boxes full of dishes and china that had lain untouched for years. This particular type of consignment rarely turns up today, though; perhaps, after seventeen years, we have emptied all the storage places in the area. Yet the merchandise still comes in from everywhere—and the greater miracle is where all of it goes. It is amazing that week after week people are willing to pay money for, and cart off, somebody else's unwanted merchandise. Part of the business is being dependent on unfortunate occurrences, like divorce, death, or bankruptcy, to create a new supply of goods.

The items are "lotted" as they come in, with a separate number given to each. The selling and listing of the items is done by the number, so that all is kept properly together. We have a big crew: a clerk, a cashier; two people to pass merchandise up to the auction stand; a "feeder," who gets items ready; and generally six runners to deliver the merchandise to the successful bidder and collect the money. Some of our known buyers run a charge account, so they can pay by one check at the end of the sale. A house or commercial auction on premises being sold out is conducted in the same manner.

Incidentally, all our five sons have started as auction runners at the age of eight, earning their own spending money. When they were little they might work for only an hour or two, and handle just the smallest items. They have enjoyed their experience, and have built good bank accounts over the years.

By having a big crew we are able to keep an auction moving, with interest high and bidding brisk. Quite often, in the case of a large auction, we can sell in one day what another auctioneer might have to use two to do. This speed is much better for the subscriber who hires the auctioneer, as the expenses are kept down. Also, prices the second day of an auction are never better than the first.

A technique we do not use is to put up the less desirable items first and save the better items for last, in the hope of keeping the dealers and buyers present. This is fatal, and you can judge how little an auctioneer knows if he does it. If he fails to put up good items for dealers, they will lose interest and go off to someone else's sale, leaving him with all the good merchandise on his hands when the only people left to bid on it are ones who either don't know what it is, or don't want it at any reasonable price. We always start with the best merchandise possible, to set the tone and the prices of the auction high; and they will stay that way all day, even when the inferior items are sold later on.

It is necessary to do a lot of outside buying in order to keep a weekly auction going, so before long I began to buy the personal property of estates, ordinary household goods, and even much new merchandise.

Remembering my father's advice about creating friendly gossip, I would search out items like hickory hammer handles. Seconds, and packed two hundred to a gunnysack, they cost us only five cents apiece; at the time, they were selling in stores for thirty-five cents each.

Holding up six, I had the bunch worked up to a dollar very quickly—a good buy for the customer and an excellent profit for me. The gossip started when I changed the deal from six for a dollar to twelve for a dollar. The crowd came off the stands for that one, and we had to dump bag after bag right on the floor in front of the auction stand so we could get them out fast enough for the customers, trusting them to give the clerks their dollars.

I have never seen such an uproar or confusion at an auction before or since. And I heard about those hammer handles for six months afterward, with written requests from miles away to mail some of them collect.

Another time, we obtained a deal on pocket combs at one cent apiece, and passed them out at twenty for a quarter. My father was in the stands that day with some friends, and after the auction he commented that we could have done much better selling six for a quarter, and had as many deals.

"How much would you gossip about six for a quarter, as against twenty for a quarter?" I asked him. He got the message.

But deals like these came with experience. More typical of the early days was the time I bought five barrels of vinegar and a five-year-old barrel of cider from a cellar in the northern part of the county. The old-timers advised against moving it, because doing so would spoil it. This was one of my first lessons in learning more about what I bought before I bought it. But I had no intention of leaving my purchase behind, so I moved it into my cellar. It lay there a year before it was tapped.

It is my understanding that a plant, called a "mother," grows inside the barrel during fermentation and should not be disturbed, but disturbing mother didn't seem to do any harm to the vinegar—and certainly not the cider, which came out bubbling like champagne. Naturally, the men at the auction heard about this, so I took down a few jugs for them to sample. Needless to say, the bidding was very spirited that day. Thereafter it became a ritual to have a few jugs on hand every Saturday until it was gone, after which the prices were not quite so good.

19

During this time, too, I had my first serious exposures to antiques.

Buying the personal effects of several estates, and selling these as well as many others consigned made it necessary for me to acquaint myself with all kinds of antiques, or else I could hope for no more. Dealers were quite fussy and all items had to be "just right" or they couldn't be sold for any price at all. Learning the degrees of condition and desirability were the greatest challenges at this time. The dealers knew their antiques, but the public didn't know much about them. The articles would be brought in by the truckful or carful from the attics and barns in the area. If I could buy back every antique I sold during the years from 1951 through 1955 at the prices they sold for then, I could retire today on the added profit that could be made at the present time.

This was the period of the buyers' market, yet the demand by the consumers and collectors was still not great enough for anyone to make a killing in them. Those were the days when heirs wouldn't want any of Grandmother's old furniture and "junk," so estates could be bought intact, and outstanding auctions could be held. Nowadays the awareness of antiques inspires most heirs to take out the most desirable pieces and have an auction with the leavings. Frank always said, "They take all the cream and leave just the skim milk."

Believe it or not, I am not opposed to this. There is something sad about people not retaining the good antiques left them. There is more written into an antique than its monetary value. There is a lot of beauty about an antique—fine ones are works of art—some may have been made by original members of the family—others were wedding gifts and have sentimental value. I don't see how people can bear to part with some of the pieces they sell, but I guess that many don't feel that the old can mix with some of the new, which is the attitude that keeps antique dealers and auctioneers in business.

You may be curious as to who gets auction fever, who consigns and buys, and why.

First, I think the auction barn serves as a meeting place for friends and families every Saturday night, where they can catch up on the news while being entertained. There are dealers in everything from antiques to near junk. There are semi-dealers whose friends ask them to pick up certain items, which they will bring home to them at a profit. There are just plain characters who come for a good time and give others a lot of laughs.

A good share of the consignors is made up of dealers who will buy out housefuls and move the prime pieces to their shops. They will have the rest sold at auction to recover the money spent for the entire load, and treat the best items as their profit. In this manner, they don't have a lot of lesser items cluttering up their shops, and they have their working capital back in hand to buy with the following week.

About half the balance of the consignors is made up equally between those who have to sell items because they need money, and those who just wish to dispose of unwanted articles. For years some families have eaten from the proceeds of consignments, as they will clean out peoples' attics and cellars at no charge—just for the contents—and bring the sellable items to the auction.

The buyers drive in from all over the country in everything from rickety old pickup trucks to Imperials. Everyone is so casually dressed that they almost all look alike. Certainly they are all treated alike.

Some good merchandise is turned away at the door because the owners want to receive a certain price for it. We explain that we conduct an auction, not a store with price tags on the goods. We then ask them if they would like to come to an auction with the feeling that they had to bid a pre-set amount for an article, or they wouldn't get it. Usually they admit the fallacy of their thinking and trust to the merchandise bringing the price it should. We have disappointed very few such consignors, as good items bring a good price and junk items bring a junk price.

Because antiquing has been found to be fun, I guess that by now it has become one of our national pastimes. In addition, it is a means of introducing things artistic to many people; all aspects of art are allied in that good imagination, good taste, and good execution are necessary if the articles are to be appreciated. But too often the heirs think that, because they have found something carved, faded, and dusty in Grandmother's attic or barn, they have found something of antique value. And this is where the interest lies in attempting to appraise and evaluate such pieces.

If you find yourself in this situation, my advice, for what it may be worth, is simple: Let your emotions be your guide on what you wish to keep. Don't hang on to pieces merely because you think they have some monetary value. It is much better to appreciate them because you like them, and can put them to some use in your home.

However, if you wish to dispose of them, and do not have enough items to warrant an appraisal, you may either sell them to a reliable dealer or consign them to a local auction house for disposal. Most states have associations of antique dealers and of auctioneers; members can put you in touch with someone reliable in your area.

I have found that in an auction ordinary merchandise will generally bring more than what one can get for it in any other manner. People who sell their goods from their garages or porches can easily be misleading themselves, because often they have little idea of values, and may be giving valuable things away at ridiculously low prices. At an auction the dealers will never let anything out for less than what is called a dealer's price, and usually this is a good price for it. Competitive bidding forces the price only one way—up; dickering forces the price only one way—down.

The novice is seldom capable of grading quality: it takes a person long years in the business to be able to do this. Yet, for most people, just the ability to recognize good workmanship and design is enough for a long time until they have a chance to learn about the fine points.

Perhaps the greatest challenge is to learn what is desirable. Without this quality, nothing has value. Creating desirability is not easy, and no one knows exactly how it is done. Still, out of nowhere fads creep in, and abruptly up goes the price on the oddest items because they suddenly become short in supply. There is resistance to too great an increase in price, though, and this will shift attention to something else. The Camp pieces that have come in strongly lately are nothing but inexpensive items from the past that were durable, on the whole are grotesque and sometimes even horrible-looking, and yet have an honest, homey quality about them that suggests life in the Good Old Days when existence was less complicated.

As for buying—which I'll talk about in detail in later chapters—the important thing again is to use what you buy. Not everyone can afford the fine early items. Appreciation of the later pieces that are within your means is at least a step in the right direction.

There is no mystery in antiquing. Like anything else, it must be learned through association, education, and the use of downright common sense. And the quickest way to learn is by buying and selling and losing money in the process, as I discovered with the help of Norman Rowe soon after I started diversifying at Barn No. 3.

Uncle Frank's brother George was nationally known as a dealer before illness had made him bedridden, and Norman, George's son, had a history in the business that extended back even before the Depression. Norman liked to tell the story on himself of an incident that took place in the early Thirties. Having acquired for a paltry sum a silver porringer dating back into the 18th century, he proceeded to ask the then tremendous price of one hundred dollars for it. A local dealer and his son, who hauled goods to New York regularly, paid him the price and took off for the big city. A week later these same dealers came back through town and saw Norman standing on a street corner. They were driving a gleaming new Chrysler and stopped to show it off. And also to thank Norman for the car: the porringer was the product of an early silversmith whose work brought big money even in depression times, and they'd sold it in New York for enough to buy their automobile.

Norman never forgot this experience, and for me it underlined the importance of studying identification. But it was in furniture that he was perhaps my greatest teacher. His favorite sport was to bring something like a lampstand to me and, on my questioning its authenticity and condition, he would proclaim all its virtues and suggest that I examine it for myself. This I would do with my limited knowledge; then, satisfied that it was perfect, I would buy it from him. Whereupon he'd laugh and crow that one leg was brand new, the brass pull wasn't old, the top had been replaced with a board of improper thickness, and on and on. These little lessons weren't too costly, however, and gradually his instructions sank in on how to recognize the good from the bad pieces. I think Norman liked me and wanted to help me learn, but wanted to get paid for doing it in a way he'd enjoy.

Along with getting to know antiques I was also getting to know the auction business, and in 1953 I was able to move from No. 3 at the fairgrounds into my own auction barn, built for me outside town in Sunset Village, and called the Strafford County Auction Exchange; the following year I added the Village Steak House in order to feed the crowds at the weekly sales. Meanwhile I was learning that to go antiquing, you must enjoy the fun of it, first and foremost. Next, you must be curious enough to study about antiques, and you must be ready to identify good from bad and consider their true worth. Then, you must be willing to explore fairly far afield for them.

And sometimes it is good to take a friend along. Frank always said, "Two liars are better than one when it comes to buying antiques." He would follow this up with: "Two heads are better than one in buying antiques, even if one is a punkin head."

3

Collecting
and Enjoying
Antiques

JUST WHAT constitutes an antique technically is something which is open to discussion; and when by "antique" it is implied that an article also possesses beauty, integrity or inherent appeal, the matter is complicated even further. So, before I go on to talk of the trends and the *what*'s and the *why*'s of antiquing as observed from personal experience, it is necessary to examine several points of view. In addition, I want to mention that, for simplicity's sake, I am concentrating on items available in America and which date back no earlier than our Pilgrim times.

One definition follows a decree by the U. S. Customs that anything a hundred years old can be considered an antique as a basis for determining duties on imports. Another rule of thumb, widely adhered to, is a former edict that the article must have been made before 1830 to qualify as an antique. Both descriptions present a number of questions that can be answered only by individual reaction—not arbitrarily.

Pre-1830—or One Hundred Years?

There are authorities who deplore the one-hundred-year yardstick, on the ground that it would bring many machine-made items into the category and thus tend to encourage these pieces to be regarded in the same light as fine handmade articles that came earlier. It is not hard to sympathize with their feeling. On the other hand, though, to accept their stand without reservation would be to exclude many satisfying items produced between 1830 and what would be at this writing the cutoff date of 1867. Such articles, and other quite valuable ones of even later times, will be noted in a moment. Certainly dealers, on the whole, should not complain about a self-adjusting rule which could open the way to creating a market for many things that have not come into favor at the present time.

It is in furniture particularly that the pre-1830 definition has the most readily perceived validity, for that time marked the beginning in America of the widespread use of power-driven tools, with resulting mass production in place of the former handcrafting. But here again the implication, not the date itself, is the important factor.

An old friend who was an antique dealer once said to me: "An antique is just like your wife—never take either for granted."

I have thought about his comment a great deal. After all, a work of art is a lifeless object; it is material, and therefore must be accorded only the regard due any material thing. To a point, this is so. Yet I know through my own experience that good antiques are not lifeless in the true sense of the word. The handmade item projects a feeling expressed by the craftsman who fashioned it, and we must recognize and appreciate this quality.

Although the article may have been produced a couple of hundred years ago, it can talk to us today in terms of fine workmanship, good taste in design and construction, and in the pleasing blends of materials that are its physical components. There are very few antique-conscious people who are not moved by the sight of an 18th-century highboy or block-front piece. Fine early silver work, carvings, homespuns, scrimshaw intrigue us with the manner in which they were made. Some of the colored glasses of the late 19th century also promote a feeling of warmth and satisfaction. All these give us great pleasure to view, as witness the success of our museums and restorations.

Can truly lifeless objects inspire so many people to esteem them? I think not; and I understand why my friend cautioned me never to take antiques for granted.

Thus, for me, the term "antique" means only those items which have handwork incorporated in their manufacture. I don't think anything stamped out by machine can have much quality or character, because there is no personal expression of artistry in it.

Nor do I think that age alone can create an antique. Something that was a monstrosity two centuries ago could very well be a monstrosity today: the years will not necessarily have done anything for it. At nearly the opposite extreme, however, are pieces made in the 1920's and '30's by craftsmen working by hand with basic tools. The taste, materials and workmanship of these articles guarantee for them an increasing value as time goes by. Almost squarely in the middle are the carved pieces of the Victorian period—often decorated with grapes or roses—which, although technically antiques by one definition, were actually cut by a powered machine that was guided by a master pattern. There is no question that there were still fine cabinetmakers carving by hand during this period, but the chance of casually running across their work is very unlikely compared with the incidence of machine-made examples.

Perhaps the best way to correlate the divergent opinions touched on so far in this discussion is to apply them by dividing the whole spectrum of antiques roughly into two types: the true antiques—which have an established value and aesthetic merit as a result of good design and good materials handled with taste, skill, and character—and the merely collectible items. All true antiques are, of course, collectible, but not all collectible objects come under my definition of antiques; certainly, machine-made items of bygone periods must be regarded only as collectible at present.

A thumbnail chronology will serve to indicate the antiques that are available, to a greater or less degree, in this country. In some cases furniture will be used as an orientation category since, interestingly, the styles of silver, glass, china, and other allied household articles adhered quite closely to the decorative touches and forms of the furniture, enough so that contemporary pieces of related items can be traced easily.

Starting only so far back as Pilgrim times in the early 1600's, we find that most of the American-made artifacts will be crude tables, sea chests, Bible boxes, and kitchen and farm utensils, usually fashioned from pine or oak. There is a good chance that many of the formal, carved oak pieces of this era came over from England, so documentation of origin is highly important.

Toward the latter part of the 17th century the heavy carved and turned furniture that is typified as Jacobean made its appearance here, but most of what we find of this must have been made in Britain. There is not an abundance of this style; neither is it in too strong demand generally, because many people find it too massive and dark to be compatible with later designs. It was followed very quickly by work representative of the William and Mary period going into the 18th century, characterized by work that was beautifully turned, and just as handsomely painted or veneered. The stretchers that went from leg to leg added strength as well as grace to the pieces.

The making of furniture really got under way at this time, and began to flourish during the Queen Anne period in the opening decades of the 18th century. This style, which extended into the mid-1700's, when the influence of Chippendale and the brothers Adam became felt, is the most highly sought after today. The Chippendale pieces command the next highest prices, followed by those of Heppelwhite design at the end of the century and the Sheraton style which was popular until about 1830. The latter two types fall into what is commonly referred to in this country as the Federal period. It is noteworthy that all these designs emanating from England dominated our modes of construction, even though Britain and the United States were politically at odds with each other for many years.

Two of the most widely known American makers of furniture, Duncan Phyfe and Lambert Hitchcock, produced in relatively large quantity for their times, mainly in the first and second quarters of the 19th century, respectively. The factory-made Hitchcock chairs have a certain amount of hand detail, and this factor and pleasing design give them a charm that is lacking in work from the heyday of the Victorian influence.

In furniture, there is a delineation that should be observed. Rural craftsmen quite often designed their pieces in very simple style, and used the local woods, with their different grainings, to achieve warmth and color. The city craftsmen, however, whose clients often were affluent ships' captains and merchants, created furniture with much more stature and design, highlighted by more handwork and carving, and with lots of inlay and veneer to heighten the color and emphasize design. We refer to these as city pieces and country pieces.

Native American glassware dates from around 1750, and that which was made right up to the end of the 19th century is highly prized, both for colored and patterned pieces. Prominent in any list of early makers are the names Stiegel and Wistar. The sixty-year production of the Boston and Sandwich Glass Company, which spanned nearly the entire Victorian era, is responsible for many millions of pieces. On the heels of Sandwich glass came the Art Nouveau work fashioned by Tiffany, which has lately come into favor with collectors.

There is relatively very little available in early American china, since our potters could not compete with foreign imports. The earliest chinas here are Chinese export porcelains and English wares made in the first half of the 18th century. Our earliest best efforts were made in Philadelphia by Tucker between 1825 and 1835. Much of this can be seen in the State Museum at Harrisburg, Pennsylvania.

In contrast, our silvermakers were prolific, and their work dates from 1700. Much early pewter has also turned up. Most of the fine early brass came from overseas, mainly England. Cast iron made in Britain and America looks very much alike.

With the exception of the furniture and silver craftsmen, who had real going businesses during the 18th century, important manufacturing did not take place until steam power had proved successful in our textile industry during the second quarter of the 19th century.

As for values, it is quite obvious that those items which, fulfilling the requirements for true antiques, have the greatest age will generally have the greatest value. One exception to this precept is furniture from Pilgrim times: although important because of age and historical association, it is very primitive and may not command prices so high as those of the fine pieces made a hundred or more years later. We consider the choice furniture to fall between the end of the 17th century and about 1830, encompassing the William and Mary through the Sheraton, or Federal, periods.

Another factor is American-made *versus* foreign-made—and this contest still goes on, with the decision in individual cases being made on the basis of personal tastes. So much was imported over the years that it would be safe to say that there are more foreign-made antique pieces in this country than native ones. If price is any indication, however, on the whole the early American items are much more valuable and will always continue to be so.

There are really so few fine such American pieces on the open market today that buyers seem to have lost their heads in their desire to possess them. A chest-on-chest-on-frame which sold in the early 1950's for the then astronomical price of $5,000, was able to command $35,000 only fifteen years later, just because it is by one of America's greatest cabinetmakers; in 1967 an English counterpart might not even bring $5,000.

Other examples abound. Our American tall clocks stand head and shoulders in value over their imported cousins because they are native to an area. Although the British clock looks similar, is just as old, runs just as well, it takes second place on the market.

Many people seem to feel that English chinas of the early 1800's, which are generally available in our shops and at auctions, would have greater worth than anything made in America. But the scarce Tucker china from Philadelphia will far exceed the prices brought today by even early Staffordshire. And a two-thousand-year-old piece of glass from overseas will arouse interest and curiosity—but just let an 18th-century piece of native Stiegel or Wistar glass come up in front of a crowd, and the bidding sails up into the stratosphere.

Appearance plays an important part, too. Usually our American furniture is much prettier than imports of comparable quality, because of the woods we used. Contrast the dark mahoganies, walnuts, and oaks of the latter with our native figured maples, birches, cherry, and lighter imported mahoganies favored by our craftsmen, and you will find American pieces on the whole have greater appeal.

The desirability of native over imported items does not hold true all over the United States, however. As only one instance, I have found that our New England pieces are frowned on in places like New Orleans and Mobile, where in colonial times the delivery of furniture, particularly, was much easier by boat from Europe than overland from the Northeast. Also, much of the background of the settlers in this area of the South was from France and Spain rather than Britain; hence the preference for items from the continent. I think people adjust themselves to the area in which they live, and desire the antiques in vogue in that area. Yet all such pieces are certainly part of America's heritage.

The best way to enjoy antiques is to use them every day and to let your own tastes prevail, for you either like something or you don't. Some people are entranced by the native, unsophisticated early pine pieces, while others want nothing less than highly refined work from the 18th century. Some homes demand English or French Provincial styles, while some tend toward the more available Empire and Victorian pieces.

It is also possible to mix styles and periods to good effect. The city and country pieces, referred to earlier, can often be combined. Good examples of furniture made between 1700 and 1830 can be mixed very gracefully indeed, even though this span embraces six different styles. Empire and Victorian pieces, unless they are the more delicate forms, would not blend happily with furniture that came before; but they can combine well with each other.

When young couples ask my advice on decoration I always tell them to furnish their apartment or house with antiques, which not only create a warmer and friendlier atmosphere than contemporary pieces do, but they also increase in value. It is really just as easy to buy an antique table, chair, chest or bed as it is to buy a new one, and quite often for less money. And in many cases antiques are much easier to care for; plus the fact that their construction and materials are such that the bumps they receive from children just add, rather than detract, from their appeal. The use of good reproductions to fill gaps when the originals can not be got makes a lot of sense, since these too will hold their value.

But what if established antiques do happen to be so scarce or so expensive that they are out of the question?

The answer is to lower one's sights and to select from what is available—but the choice should be made on the basis of merit and not merely to follow a current fad.

A fellow auctioneer told me recently of coming across an advertisement of the 1920's which announced an auction in which the headlined items were oak and mahogany pieces of the day. Beneath the boldface type was the much smaller, and casual, mention that also to be sold were some highboys, bowfront chests, slant-top desks, and old glass and china. It is difficult to believe that fine early pieces were ever held in so little regard, but as an auctioneer I still must be charitable toward the items I do not value lest they be in demand tomorrow.

For example, to me there is little inherent quality in the mission oak furniture of the early 20th century which is a paraphrase of the Spanish Colonial period. But in certain parts of the country it has become fashionable and is much in demand, although it is still inexpensive to buy (and I think should remain so). In much of New England these pieces are being broken up for firewood. In the same vein, I bemoan the fact that many dozen round oak dining tables found their way into our barrel stoves to warm an auction crowd on a Winter's night, for up to a few years ago we couldn't get even a fifty-cent bid on them.

Another item is the iron or so-called brass bedstead that is being glorified, at this writing, in magazine articles on decorating. Again as an auctioneer, I am all for publicity that will turn trash into treasure, but these beds continue to end up in town dumps. The public will always make up its own mind about things of this sort.

On the other hand, in my opinion the importance of seeking out pine furniture, especially in New England, is still underestimated. Too many people native to this region continue to

A Trove of New England Pine

regard pine as the "hired hand's furniture," and decorate with it quite sparingly. The best prices for these articles are paid by out-of-staters, who prize them and use them in their homes. Pine is still very inexpensive, yet it reflects a period of Americana when comfortable household appointments were made with a readily available raw material.

Most of the pine left here dates from the Victorian period, and the pieces in greatest demand are those from bedroom sets, the lift-top commodes, and three- and four-drawer chests. The spool lampstands, washstands, beds and chairs still go begging at auctions. Occasionally these sets are decorated with oil paintings on the head- and footboards. Quite often, itinerant artists would arrive at a farm and paint scenes of the buildings and surroundings on this furniture, therefore much of it is enhanced by this addition of primitive art. The stenciling and feather-painting found on some sets reflect a different yet beautiful approach to decoration.

Many people feel they must totally refinish these pine pieces to the natural wood, a step which can sometimes spoil their interesting look. Almost without exception, these pieces were stained or painted originally, and hence it is very proper and in keeping to paint and decorate them again. Taking pine down to the bare wood can often leave only light wood that seems too much like new, and if it is refinished with nothing but a natural finish the antique appearance would be in good measure destroyed. Recommendations for refinishing pine will be presented in another chapter.

Up to this point I have been talking about what I feel are true antiques, with the emphasis on furniture and the enjoyment derived from living with it and using it in one's home. Now, in turning to what I earlier called collectibles, I shan't try to maintain the distinction between the truly antique and the merely "period" items; nor, except occasionally in passing, will

I bother with relative importance or inherent values. And, because certain items—silver, particular glass and pottery wares and other household items, guns, jewelry, etc., etc.—are already established as collectors' fields, I am limiting my suggestions to a few areas that I know to be comparatively unexplored and therefore likely to offer good hunting and good bargains.

Some people collect as an investment and make money at it, but do so in a manner that leaves them little enjoyment. Then there are others who give in to the universal urge to collect for its own sake, and the result is shelves crammed with things that are brought out once in a while to be shown off, and then are returned to limbo. Collecting like this serves one good purpose, though: it keeps the auctioneers healthy, as we wouldn't know what to do with many items unless they were bought by people badly bitten by the collecting bug. Rather than stuff cupboards with cream pitchers, salts and peppers, and the like, how much more pleasure they would get from buying various decorative old objects that could be used at different times in different rooms!

If you wanted to start collecting as a serious pastime, and wondered what to go in for, I should advise you against meaningless curiosities, fads, and items entirely made by machine. Then, since it is easier to collect articles that are reasonably plentiful, I would direct you to things that were made in abundance, or were made in a time more recent than you at first were considering. And I would recommend, as a greatly satisfying project, searching out and preserving items that may have only regional interest and favor today, because they will be highly regarded tomorrow. Finally, I would tell you that, by applying good judgment and selectivity, you will be building a collection with definite resale value; and even if you have no intention of selling it, you will enjoy it more if you know that it has some antique value, per se.

Unless you are a dealer and know exactly what you are doing, you should never be swayed by tastes that are not your own. This is especially true if you merely follow a fancy, for they come and go, and something that is currently a find may turn out before too long to be a candidate for the rummage sale or even the junkpile. Milk glass has seen this rise and fall, and that horror of horrors, carnival glass, is destined for the back of the cupboard again some day. The vogue for collecting what is called Camp antiques has risen a great deal in the mid-1960's, but these articles should be considered for their function, rather than for any particular increment in value. Leaded oyster-shell glass lamps, a product of the early 1900's, are finding favor as amusing nowadays, but most are atrocious-looking. Yet there are some less publicized collections of fans, miniature paintings, bells, stereoscope viewers and cards that have much quality and a lot of stories to tell. There are also collections which were gathered to show the outpourings of one concern during its entire existence; an outstanding example of this sort of thing is Sandwich glass.

Among several areas of collecting that remain open without too much expense but offer a future from the standpoint of possible resale at a profit, the foremost is bottles.

Bottle collectors have been with us for a long time, but the great upsurge seemed to come right after I did two television programs which were shown coast to coast back in 1964. The classifications of the bottles, plus the discussion on their designs, age, and color, brought a response that exceeded any we had ever before received, judged by the demand for the reading lists prepared for each show and sent free on request.

In addition to descriptions, I explained that anyone could dig for this buried treasure in old dumps, especially—and of course with permission—those near old farmhouses in the country.

Out of the programs came many good stories that viewers have written me. One of the girls from Alfred, Maine, who lent me bottles for those early programs, told me she had dug up human bones while searching near Poland Spring. The police were called in on this one.

Another viewer, digging at the site of her grandparents' homestead, came across a diary preserved in a metal box, which revealed many rakish skeletons in the family closet. One man wrote that he had located a cache of old coins which must have been inadvertently thrown out sometime after 1900, as the newest coin was dated then. Needless to say, the value of these coins rewarded him for his day's work.

Digging is truly a coast-to-coast sport, since many of the finest collectible bottles date after California's 1848 gold rush opened the West. It has been said that in some of the old Western ghost towns bottles have been discovered in colors unmatched by those found anywhere else, as the result of lying for years and years in the desert sun. It would be difficult to say that one part of the country is any better to dig in, however, as bottles were spread about wherever people went. So the whole country is your area for this collecting.

Another sleeper I foresee is the collection of china and glass commemorative and lithographed pieces. On the china will show specific landmarks like town halls, churches, fairgrounds, covered bridges, and main streets or other scenes of interest in many communities. These were made mostly between 1900 and 1906, and were mainly the result of efforts by clever German chinamakers, who sent salesmen to comb this country and interest local china and gift shops in ordering such souvenir items made especially for them and quite often with the name of the store stamped on them. This last touch must have appealed to the vanity of the storekeepers, as the country was flooded with such items as cream pitchers, vases, cups and saucers, plates, etc. —but all done very well in fine quality porcelains and bone. These were followed by some rather shoddy imitations made in this country of plain crockery.

The imported pieces sold very well. They are desired today by collectors usually for historical value, as they picture scenes that are not with us today and sometimes commemorated local anniversaries or celebrations. They act almost as an historical account of the life and times of a community, and this and the fact that they really are such fine pieces of china make them quite desirable. A fad for collecting these items has not yet hit, and most can be had in auctions for less than a dollar, and in shops for a little more. But the day will come when many people will crowd this bandwagon.

Another item not much exploited at this writing is the fan. Fans made for ladies of the courts of Europe or for the wealthy in this country can truly be works of art. Many of the fine imported ones are hand-painted. The ivory ones are generally carved by hand, and show some of the finest craftsmanship I have seen, with the execution of detail always very delicate. The artisans spared no effort in exploring ideas, materials and decorations: some were made in ebony, tortoise shell, mahogany, gold, silver and other materials, which lent themselves to good design. My favorites are those designed with imperceptible slits in them so Madame could spy on the goings-on around her without showing her curiosity. Another type has a small mirror embedded in it to enable a lady to note the antics of husband or lover while her back was turned toward him.

The few collectors I know of don't stuff their finds in drawers or cabinets, but frame and hang them on the wall just as one might use a delightful painting to decorate a room. The idea of a room done in this fashion, with the many varied types of fans in different colors and designs, is very likely to encourage other people to start searching for them. And the amazing fact is that the current price I have seen for most fans is still very low, and so can enable you to capture them before the demand begins.

Collecting old books is an area in which too few people are

well versed. I find that the majority of the public whom I see do not know what constitutes value in books, and therefore quite often let good buys go to others who do know. There are no simple rules in any type of collecting, but there is one basic similarity: the law of supply and demand applies; and most books are in great supply and little demand. The remainder includes town and county histories and atlases, and of course, first editions of desirable works. Early histories and geographies and gazetteers are used by attorneys, students, and writers as sources of historical fact. For instance, I don't know an attorney who does not have an old atlas of the place where he practices, as a ready reference in researching original or early owners and old-time descriptions of properties. Even the most plentiful county histories command prices of twenty to fifty dollars in my locale, and some of them much more. Town histories often go begging at auctions, yet very few of them are worth less than ten dollars and I have seen them sold for as high as one hundred and fifty.

Of importance to us in New Hampshire is the three-volume *History of New Hampshire* by Jeremiah Belknap. His first writings were dated 1794 and were compiled and printed in 1812, along with a map dating back to 1792. Those with the map have greater value. The last set I saw sold, in 1955, brought one hundred and fifty dollars. Today, who knows what they are worth? Copies of the 1817 *Gazetteer of the State of New Hampshire* by Eliphalet and Phineas Merrill are practically extinct. This three-volume effort makes note of works dealing with New Hampshire by Winthrop, Morton, Mather, Prince, Hutchinson, Morse, and Parish, and leads the "book bug" into an interesting search for copies of their writings. These two examples are offered to point up that book-collecting is interesting, of historical importance, and very rewarding. And tangibly rewarding, too—my set of Belknap was bought in a bookstore in Schenectady, New York, for $17.50, and the Merrill *Gazet-*

Different atmospheres but similar techniques: selling a hard-to-come-by Shaker ladderback chair at a home auction, and (below) the author acknowledging bids during the Carnegie Museum's annual benefit sale.

Widely collectible are stone crocks and jugs, and bottles like (below, from left) Dr. Wistar's Balsam of Wild Cherry, Buffalo Lithia Water, Warner Safe Kidney & Liver Cure, Atwood's Jaundice Bitters, Smith's Green Mountain Renovator, and one marked "H&H, Dover, N. H."

In addition to primitive oils, old lithographs and prints of animals and marine and historic scenes are good buys. The vogue for Camp items includes bowl-and-pitcher sets, gingerbread clocks, lamps with oyster-shell leaded shades (but better is the little pine dropleaf table).

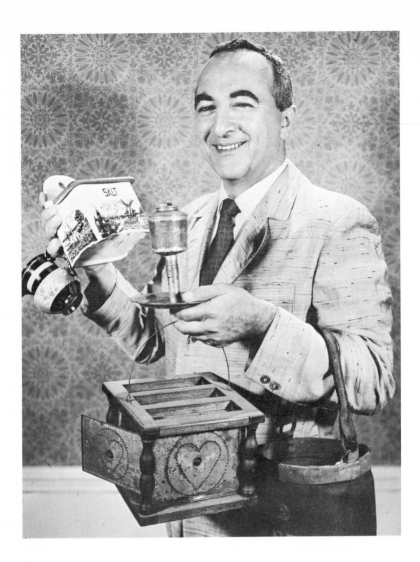

Copper luster pitcher, Delft salt box, whale-oil lamp, charcoal foot-warmer, and leather fire bucket—none of these is rare, but all are good-quality collectibles that will increase in value.

On the set of Antiques, holding a Stoddard (N. H.) demijohn, with Moses bottles and containers for Poland Spring Water on the tiger-maple side table (which is circa 1720).

45

From Philip Hammerslough's famed collection of colonial silver are the tureen made in 1782 by Peter Getz of Lancaster, Pa., and the chafing dishes by John Burt of Boston (1690-1745).

Richard Carter Barret, the foremost authority on Bennington pottery and porcelain, with only a fraction of the Bennington Museum's unequaled collection. Examples of his refreshing approach are mentioned in Chapter 9.

From the family album: the home in Rochester, N. H., and Bette with the five young Michaels (left to right, Geoffrey, Gerald, Glenn, Gary and Gregory).

teer set came in a box of books I bought for two dollars at an auction.

Just because a book is one hundred years old does not give it value. Most of the schoolbooks of the 19th century have little value. Old Bibles are so numerous that generally it is necessary to go back into the early 18th century for any with monetary value—unless, of course, they are copies with historical or personal associations that make them unusual. However, first editions can be worthwhile even when the copies are not in the antique category, but title and author must be in demand.

Among good guides as to value are the continuously updated *American Book-Prices Current,* and other sales and auction records, together with catalogs issued by antiquarian book dealers. The safest area for a novice, until he becomes quite learned, is that of histories and atlases.

Old woodenware—often called treenware in bygone years—is interesting and collectible, but is of questionable value. Such items from Grandmother's kitchen and from around the farm are good as curiosity and decorative pieces, but represent nothing into which you should put too great an investment. Some of the larger kitchen pieces like hewn chopping bowls, bowls carved from burl, unusual milk churns, and the like can be used today for their original purposes, or merely for pleasant atmosphere. Not all antiques must be functional to be enjoyed, but those we can use should be desired most. Nutmeggraters, apple-peelers, and breadboards too small for our present-day loaves only take up space, and some day will find themselves on the expendable list when the lady of the house needs a few extra dollars.

Few articles add more luster and warmth to a home than do well-chosen paintings, but unfortunately few of us can afford originals by well-established artists, let alone the works of old masters. However, the demand has not yet caught up with the supply of primitive oil paintings. This is a very fertile and rewarding field for collection, enjoyment, and investment, particularly if the subjects are from one's own area.

Even as recently as the latter half of the 19th century, there were artists who traveled throughout the Northeastern countryside in search of commissions to record local scenes for posterity in work which often rivaled that of sophisticated city painters of the times. Most of them, described as belonging to the White Mountain or Hudson River schools of painting, were devoted to realism to the point of being almost photographic in detail. Also, well into this century, a number of such painters would set up studios near well-known areas drawing summer visitors from many parts of the country, and quite often would paint a sample scene and take orders for ones like it in specific sizes. Then, when the tourist season was over, they would retire to their own homes to paint however many copies had been ordered. This practice accounts for the number of pictures of the White Mountains, the Catskills and the Adirondacks that turn up far away in the Midwestern and Western states.

In addition, it was not unusual for itinerant portrait painters of the 1700's and 1800's to spend the long Winters painting bodies on individual canvases, omitting the heads. Then during the warm months they would journey from town to town, looking for families who would engage them to paint likenesses by merely adding the heads and features of the sitters. Some of these "instant" portraits seem rather odd by our standards today, but apparently they were accepted then; and the result was interesting genre art.

It was not too long ago that primitive oils were bought only for the frames that housed them. Not so today, however, even though old portraits still go begging at auctions and in shops because "they are somebody else's relatives, so why should we buy them?" The answer is that, as in the case of museums, these should be shown as representative of the period involved.

Documentation and Appraisal

If you wish to begin collecting primitives, my first advice is to start with paintings from your own area done by local artists, and then branch into the works of more widely known painters, within the limits of your pocketbook. From the standpoint of enjoyment, primitives can be among the most charming acquisitions for your home.

An important part of owning antiques is the preparation for disposing of them in the future by gift, bequest, or sale, so I offer the following suggestions as a corollary to the discussion of collecting.

Why not take time to write down all you know about the pieces you own? The maker, either individual or concern; the date of manufacture; the original buyer; sales slips, if possible, showing the transaction; who has owned it since; the date it came into your possession, and the price you paid—all these are important to future owners and certainly are important for tax purposes. When a craftsman put his touchmark, stamp or label on a piece, he insured greater value for it today because collectors pay more for items like this. The fact that items were owned by famous people or even used by famous people enhances their value. A lot of times heirs do not know the true value of antiques and sell them for little or nothing.

Appraisal, which will help in your documentation, is also important. Plan to have this done soon as a base for future evaluations of your estate. Most banks that have a trust department and most attorneys utilize the services of competent appraisers in estate settlement, and it is possible to secure the name of such qualified people from either source.

Some people shrink at the mention of the cost of an appraisal, yet I have never seen a situation yet where an appraiser did not earn his day's pay on a single item. I did an appraisal way up in Maine several years ago, and while going through the house with me the owner was growling about how much this service was costing him. Coming into his living room, I spied a piece of furniture, which shall remain unidentified, and he remarked that this was a very good piece. I asked him how good he thought it was, and he stated emphatically that the piece would never leave his home for less than two thousand dollars, expecting to shock me with this figure. I asked him if he would sell it for two thousand dollars that day, and he said he would. Thereupon I showed him the appraisal figure of eight thousand dollars I had written down, and reminded him that if I were not there to appraise, I really could have made some money. The growling stopped.

Appraisal is also important for insurance purposes and for arriving at tax deductions for gifts to charities or certain non-profit institutions. A lady donated a fine furniture piece to a worthwhile charity and had listed its value at three hundred dollars, the price which she had paid some years before. While assisting in selling the item, I told her that this figure was unrealistic, as its current value was nearer seven hundred. I wrote her a letter so stating, and she was able to claim this larger deduction.

Still another benefit of appraisal is that it makes for an orderly distribution of antiques to children during one's lifetime. Because it is possible to make gifts up to three thousand dollars a year with no tax encumbrance on the recipient, people can plan to give antiques up to this value yearly to their children, so that on death these items are no longer part of the donor's estate. A recipient must take the pieces into his own home, as they can not remain with the donor. In today's rising price market such a dispersal can have an important effect on the taxes and fees paid by an estate.

4

Matters of

Identification

SOME YEARS AGO, Norman Rowe, Kippy Carswell—another dealer—and I went to a church benefit auction where Chuck Emmons, the noted auctioneer from Sanbornville, New Hampshire, was in action.

He was spreading antiques all over the crowd with his rapid chant, and soon a fine round-cornered lift-top commode was brought up. It was in several pieces, though: the top was off, the upper section separated from the lower; the door was off, and the skirt was loose. My bid of three-fifty won it for me and the helpers brought it to where we stood.

Kippy looked it over and said, "George, I like that commode —I'll give you five dollars for it."

"Give me your change," I told him. "I haven't soiled my hands, and I'll take a quick profit."

He paid me.

A few minutes later Norman said to him, "I'll give you a profit on that commode, Kip. Would you take six dollars for it?"

Money exchanged hands again, and we loaded the thing into the car to start for home. As we discussed the auction, I mentioned to both of them that they had taken advantage of me, and I offered Norman eight dollars for the commode. He took the money, and we arrived at Milton Mills.

Just as Kip was getting out of the car, he took out a ten-dollar bill. "George," he offered, "here's ten dollars for the commode before you take off."

He owned it once more; and that night he got out a hammer and nails and put it together.

The next day Chuck Emmons was making his rounds to pick up antiques for his regular Saturday auction. He stopped to buy from Kip and noticed the commode. Not recognizing it as the one he had sold the day before for three-fifty, he gave Kip twelve-fifty for it—only to sell it two days later for eighteen dollars.

All of which proves that to buy antiques effectively, in the rough, one must have imagination and knowledge of identification.

One must learn to recognize quality and value regardless of condition, or layers of paint, or other disguises that have been added to a piece down through the years. Many times one will see the top half of a chest-on-chest with legs or base mounted to serve as a single chest. A dealer I know bought a boxful of parts and pieces for half a dollar; when put together they turned out to be a beautiful melodeon made in Concord, New Hampshire, in 1849.

Many of the clues used in identifying antiques are simple and, once learned, are very obvious. For instance, the age of a Windsor chair can be judged fairly accurately by the width of the splay in the legs: the wider the splay, the older the chair. Nor is it difficult to learn whether a board has been cut by hand by a two-man jacksaw, or by a powered circular saw, since the marks left by each can readily be identified. The width of teeth in dovetailing and the number of them can furnish a clue as to age, because the wider, cruder cuts are generally older. The thickness of the top of a four-legged lamp or candlestand will help determine authenticity, as those made of hardwood rarely have a thickness over five-eighths of an inch.

Mavericks and Ones-of-a-kind

Items like silver and pewter most often carry their maker's touchmark, which makes identification easy. Not all old china or glass is marked, so this is much more difficult to pin down.

Cast iron is most difficult to identify, because some that was made but a few years ago can, if dusty and well rusted, fool a majority of us. Not long ago in an auction I sold a large iron school-bell for forty-two dollars and fifty cents. It came out of a barn in a box, but looked a hundred years old. I noticed a stock number on the box and later checked it in the Sears catalog. There I learned that the bell could be bought at the time for twenty-seven-fifty; and since the stock numbers coincided, this must have been relatively a new one.

We had a fine cabinetmaker in town by the name of Albert Gile. Albert was one of a dwindling school of craftsmen who spent years as an apprentice to an old German cabinetmaker in Dover. Quite often he would walk the ten miles to get to his work and back again that night. The devotion to his education resulted in workmanship that could be duplicated by very few, and he was sought by dealers and collectors from miles around to do repair work and to make reproductions. We have in our home a Hepplewhite banquet table made by him, and which was labeled by Israel Sack, the dean of American antique dealers, as "the finest piece of New Hampshire craftsmanship I have ever seen."

One thing that Albert used to do quite often was add long slender posts to the lower four-posted maple beds to make canopy tops out of them. His work was so fine that I have never seen one of his remade beds challenged.

Norman Rowe had a bed made over into a four-poster and set up in his room, and he used it while waiting for the right time to sell it. One day an old dealer friend of his drove into the yard. Norman said to his housekeeper, "Tell him I'm sick. I'm getting into bed."

Then he stripped off his shirt and jumped into bed with

55

his shoes and pants still on. The dealer came in, inquired after his health, and carried on a light conversation—all the while eyeing the bed.

"Norman," he said finally, "this has gone on long enough. You know I want that bed you're in."

Feigning shock, Norman replied, "Why, you wouldn't buy the bed out from under a sick man, would you?"

"Yes, I would," answered the dealer. "I'll give you three hundred for it."

At this point Norman weakly accepted the money. Once it was in his hands he jumped out of bed, clothed as he was, and exulted: "You damn fool, those posts had leaves on them only six weeks ago!"

I understand the dealer still laughs about this one to this day. As Uncle Frank always said, "It pays to get beat once in awhile. It just sharpens you up."

This goes to show that one should not buy in haste without some examination, especially when lots of money changes hands.

Layers of paint and varnish hide beautifully grained woods and contrasting woods used on many early pieces. A pine top with a scroll back on a lowboy having Queen Anne legs is enough to confuse anybody until he gets underneath to examine the construction; then he finds the rasp marks on the cabriole legs, and the crude long pegs used during that period to join the legs and sides. Whereupon it becomes obvious that at some time this was the base for a highboy, and someone during the late Sheraton or early Empire period put on a suitable top for the times in order to convert it into a lowboy.

About the best way to determine age and authenticity of most pieces is to look at them from underneath. If there was any damage to a piece, generally it would be in the base or leg construction; and therefore it is here that the restoration or reconstruction shows up. One must study and learn what a piece should look like in order to determine authenticity.

Authenticity from Underneath

Our many fine books on antiques help us in this, for identification of a period is important. Too many writers stop there, though, and don't examine the qualities of each type. This lack prompts a suspicion that an author may be doing nothing more than rehashing other people's writings, plus adding a little knowledge of his own. The categorizing of the good, better, and bests in antiques is an ability that only experience can give a person. Thus, books that merely identify period are not enough.

As an example, let us examine lift-top commodes. These are a product of our mid-19th-century Victorian period. The pine pieces of the period are referred to as cottage or camp furniture. The pine bedroom sets of that era generally consisted of a high-back bed, painted or stenciled; four-drawer bureau; dresser with mirror—some with a deep well, others in four-drawer fashion with small side drawers on top; lift-top commode, in which the wash basins and other receptacles were kept; a curved-back, or Lincoln, rocker with caning on seat and back; several straight-back caned chairs; and a lampstand with or without drawer.

It is of interest to note that some say this is the only furniture style native to this country. However, one must note the overtones of Scandinavian and Nordic design.

To identify the most desirable lift-top, here are some tips: It must be of solid pine single-board construction; thickness must be one inch, or, as planed boards, three quarters of an inch; sides must be solid; corners must be rounded; it must have a single drawer with an appropriate pull, either a wooden carved knob, acorn-carved, or teardrop handle; single door; and gracefully cut skirt on front and sides.

Less desirable pieces have plain knob, paneled sides, square corners, two-board construction in top or sides, no drawers, double door, straight skirt, and are made of a wood other than pine. I have seen them in walnut and mahogany, designed to go with the heavy Victorian bedroom sets; also in ash, oak and poplar. I have never seen one in birch, maple or cherry, which were some of our most popular early woods.

Occasionally we find a Pennsylvania or New York piece with lift top, double doors, and large bottom drawer. These are larger than our New England pieces, and have squared corners and straight skirts.

Other points of less importance are the desirability of dovetailed drawers as against doweled ones; square-cut nails as against more rounded ones; hewn or sawed boards in the back; early eye-hinges; spool-carved split columns to decorate the front corners.

If you find one with the original paint or stencil and it is in good condition, it will have more value if you leave it that way. Other than that, refinishing is very much in order, with feather-painting design, paint or stencil applied. These pieces were not sold finished in their natural tones, so colors, stencils, and designs are in perfect keeping.

These pine pieces—even *in* pieces—can provide you with interesting antiques, are very plentiful and inexpensive in New England, and are very easy to live with. This is truly comfortable furniture and quite easy to identify.

New Englanders, especially those from Cape Cod, are proud of the heritage of glass-making concerns which spread the fame of the Yankee craftsmen throughout the world. The Boston and Sandwich Glass Company, which was founded by Deming Jarves in 1825 in Sandwich on the Cape, is perhaps the most famous of them all.

Unfortunately as a result of fact or fiction, most glass made during the 1800's—especially the pressed pieces—has been attributed to this company. To identify all such old glass as Sandwich is one of the greatest errors being made today by dealers and collectors alike. Documentation is the only sure way to identify the glass, along with their unique patterns.

Problems with Glasswares

The New England Glass Works, East Boston Glass Works, and Mount Washington Glass Works of Boston and New Bedford were contemporary with the Sandwich concern, and the outpourings from these and many other New England-based works were so much alike that even persons regarded as experts would be hard put to identify positively the place of manufacture. Artisans would travel from plant to plant working with the same techniques, ideas, and designs and quality of glass, so that it is next to impossible to tell where they did their work. Since there were other famous glass works like those in New Jersey and Pittsburgh and Portland, Maine, and all these companies shipped their wares across the country and to other parts of the world, one is likely to find examples of their craftsmanship everywhere.

The Sandwich concern had a big distribution center in San Francisco, and today one may find almost as much true Sandwich glass there as here in the East. So the next time someone holds up a piece of glass and identifies it as Sandwich, don't hesitate to ask for documentation. You'll be respected for your thoroughness rather than be ignored for your impertinence.

The Sandwich Glass Museum houses an elegant display of both clear and colored glass that will delight anyone. Many people are under the impression that only clear glass, such as in the pressed pieces, was made at Sandwich. The museum disproves this, with some of the most exciting colored-glass work one will ever see.

It is a challenge to the layman to figure out how many of these items were made. The delicate shadings of color into color, some cut, some molded, arouse the curiosity of those interested in all phases of antiques. The display of blowpipes, pattern molds, shears, and other tools of the trade makes us wonder how such classic pieces could be turned out with such primitive devices. The factory flourished throughout the 19th century and was credited with originating many designs and styles, among them the delicate Mary Gregory glass. This is the application of an overlay design of white glass on colored bases with scenes involving people and animals. Caught up in the increasing pressures exerted by labor reform and competition, the company was hard put to stay in business. Finally in 1885 the plant was closed. There were two attempts to revive the operation, but these, too, were unsuccessful.

I should guess that the identification of old glass has proved the greatest challenge to buyers. Even museum curators show a reluctance to document pieces unless they are positive of their origin. It is not too difficult to classify old glass so far as age and construction are concerned, which is a help in building clues as to its origin. But, the fact that all the companies did such similar work, while copying each other's designs, makes it next to impossible to be very definite in opinion. Appraising this is not too difficult, for, with the exception of some designs and some work by known craftsmen, the values would be much alike; thus place of manufacture is relatively unimportant.

Most chinas, silver, and pewter were marked in some manner. Many books have been printed showing the marks on these items, and so make identifying them relatively easy. The fine early silver craftsman, whether English or American, would stamp his name or initials along with some personal touchmark on the bottoms of his pieces. Pewterers would do the same thing. No imports into America had to be marked to show country of origin until 1892, when our country passed a law requiring foreign exporters to identify their wares as a protection to American producers.

Documenting some of these wares can be difficult, too, as much that was made before 1892 would be stamped so it could be exported here, so using just this stamp as a guide for dating a piece can be hazardous. Also, in the early days the American craftsmen in china didn't want to identify their wares: the foreign imports commanded better prices, and the domestic producers often left theirs unmarked so they might be mistaken for imports. Many of the early chinas were marked from England, especially during the Staffordshire period in the 1820's and 1830's, because the companies took pride in their work and wanted to be identified with their pieces.

One must learn to tell old china from new just by looking at it. Different shapes and forms turned up during different periods, and hence this can be a guide. Decorations changed, so the changes can be an indication during a period. One difficulty in nailing down particular years of manufacture is that a concern might make a pattern for fifty or more years in exactly the same manner.

Fine quality cut glass is often etched with the maker's name in such a manner that one is obliged to hold it to the light at the right angle in order to see it.

If you have any pewter with the word "pewter" spelled out on the bottom, this is not collectible as it is too new.

Appraisal of the early Chinese export porcelains is not easy unless one studies them closely. This type of ware arrived in England and here in abundance from the early 1700's, so there is a good deal of it still in existence despite its age. However, so much of it was made in the same design for over a hundred years that documenting true age must be left to an expert. What is most important to the beginner is to be able to tell one china from another, and at least be able to identify the country of origin. This is not too difficult, but one must go to museums to see the pieces, and read good books that tell the stories about them.

A lot of people buy by name alone and want only specific items. Particular craftsmen are selected, generally because of regional interest, and collectors will concentrate only on their works. They feel they are doing a real service in assembling the works of a particular man, so the broad scope of his artistry may be appreciated. This type of collecting presents a very worthwhile plan for antiquing, as there are too few people who can identify unmarked items, yet those who have studied the fine details of craftsmanship can often pinpoint a maker just by his work.

Wherever I travel around the country, I urge people to collect items made locally so that the history of the area may be preserved. This type of collecting is much more interesting than the random acquisition of objects having few, if any, regional associations. Soon you will be able to identify the items you see with no trouble, and be able to show and talk about them to local groups. Many people have also done well financially from such an effort.

I mentioned in the preceding chapter that documenting antiques is important, and I bring it up again now in connection with identifying the work of individuals. People often tell me that dealers tell them they cannot buy and sell sentiment, so what difference does it make whether they know that Great-grandfather made a chest of drawers? All I can say is that the unknown maker of today may be famous tomorrow. If enough pieces by the same maker keep turning up, and the work is good, then demand is created; hence all the pieces may be worth more.

I remember selling Tiffany vases in the early 1950's for from three to five dollars, yet today their prices have gone out of sight because of a new appreciation of the work of this man. The work done by Harold Kendall in Surrey, New Hampshire, in locating and documenting the Hampshire pottery made by the J. S. Taft Company in Keene, has resulted in a fine collection of pieces that have risen in value because of interest and the demand created for them. Harold has written a pamphlet on this pottery, and is much sought after as a speaker.

Such avenues of worthwhile exploration are open to all. So look around locally for an interesting and rewarding experience in identifying and collecting native craftsmanship.

5

Bidding
at Auctions

GEORGE THOMPSON was one of the first New Hampshire auctioneers I had met. He passed away several years ago at the
age of eighty-five, perhaps the oldest working auctioneer in the
country at the time. He had done an auction just three weeks
before his death.

His favorite expression when selling clothing was: "I have
three changes of clothing—put on, take off, and go without."
This used to shock some of the knitters and sitters in the front
row at his auctions if they were newcomers or tourists, but
they learned quickly that they were hearing one of the few
true old-timers in action, with lots of country sayings thrown
in. Holding up some ladies' unmentionables and being asked
the size, his only comment would be, "They're big enough to
fit a Jersey cow."

Perched on his tall stool under a huge wagon umbrella, he
was the epitome of auctioneers of the old school, who would
take all day to sell what we newcomers sell in a few hours. The
older folks liked his leisurely pace, though, because it gave
them time to sit and visit with their neighbors without missing

too much of what was going on. His pace was about thirty to forty items an hour, whereas in our consignment selling, with but a few hours to dispose of a barnful (about the equivalent of two housefuls) of merchandise, we go at a pace that nears the hundred mark per hour. This speed requires the attention of bidders, so no one can afford to visit or go to sleep if he is there to buy.

There are two styles of auctioneering. In the style favored by most to get the crowd bidding, an auctioneer will ask for a certain amount as a starting bid. If he doesn't receive this bid, he will drop the asking amount until someone signals him the first bid. Some feel this is instant appraisal by an auctioneer, in that he is asking at first for the amount he feels the items should bring. Don't rely on this idea, as a good auctioneer will vary his technique so rapidly that you will never catch up with him.

Other auctioneers are content to let the crowd give them the starting bid. This method also has its pitfalls, since a heckler can cause havoc and disrupt an otherwise good sale. One pulled this on me several times, with opening bids of half-dollars on the items put up, regardless of their value. Then I dumped an empty box on him for his half-dollar in the middle of a lot of fine glassware he was trying to cut down in bids, and he fell for it. This was the last of him for the day.

Many years ago another heckler fell for an old routine that we dig out from time to time. A chamber pot was sold to a pleasant woman for only fifty cents; this was despite my pleadings that it was worth more, made to the man who had been giving me a hard time all day. He remarked that it was a piece of junk, etc., until I said "Sold!" and tipped it over to allow a five-dollar bill to fall out of it to the ground below. Naturally the buyer was delighted; and the heckler was jeered off the grounds. My "feeder" had slipped the bill in at the right time to make sure the right person got it. The price of chamber pots went much higher for the ensuing weeks, so we got the five back without too much effort.

Another troublemaker fell for a real old chestnut. A box was put up and the crowd was told the truth about it—that its contents cost one hundred and twenty-five dollars, and were still brand new, never used, and in perfect condition. This "smart" buyer, who had been trying to cut bids down for the first hour, sensed a sleeper and paid nine dollars for it, as I sold it to him the moment he jumped into the bidding. He was rewarded with a set of false teeth and the hoots and howls of the crowd.

Another technique an auctioneer will use to stimulate a crowd to bid is one that can be debated. Holding up an item that he knows should bring a certain amount of dollars, he may rattle along that he has an opening bid of so many dollars on it, and call for the next bid. Many people are hesitant to give an opening bid, but will jump in once it has started. I do not consider this a deception, for in effect the auctioneer is doing the whole crowd a favor by keeping the auction moving, and doing the job for the subscriber who has hired him. If he uses his head in the instant appraisal of an item and knows its current worth, rarely will he be caught without a second bid.

A man who is just as important to the auction as the auctioneer is the man who feeds him the merchandise—commonly known as the auction manager. It is his job to describe the condition of the item; watch the crowd and notice the items they want to bid on; feed the right items to the auctioneer at the right time for the best prices; take care of buyers who have to leave and want an item up; know when to pass out a duplicate item after the price has been set on the first one sold; keep the runners active; point out bids to the auctioneer, and buyers to the runners; signal for the next items to be sold, and so on. It is his job, also, to know when friend auctioneer is hung up on his first bid: at which time he will add more items to the original until a second bid is received. This can be done so casually that the crowd will never know, as adding items is done all the time.

George Thompson used to like to tell the following story about an auction near Laconia. It was a very hot day, the bidders were sluggish, and he had a big houseful to dispose of. To get things moving he used the opening-bid technique, and was getting along fine until he held up a good old violin and asked for a two-dollar bid to start, said he had it, and went on from there. Even though the item was worth more, he could not elicit his second bid to sell it. His feeder was getting lunch, and there was no one to help him out.

A heckler in the crowd demanded to know who had placed the first bid, and he was reminded that an auctioneer never has to reveal his bidders. The heckler challenged this statement and declared that unless the bidder were revealed, and he felt there was none, he would be off for the sheriff. Just then a sweet lady in her seventies stood up and said she had given George the bid, and proceeded to berate the heckler so much he beat a hasty retreat with the applause of the crowd for his tormenter ringing in his ears. After the auction ended, she waited until the crowd had left and came up to George and handed him the violin.

"I don't really need this," she said; "you can have it back. But today you gave me the opportunity to do something I've always wanted to—to give somebody hell in public, and get away with it."

George prized that violin for many years after.

One of the greatest complaints we hear from auction-goers is that dealers buy all the good antiques. They believe the dealers outbid them on all the good pieces, and so make it almost impossible for them to bid. Reasoning like this is as hollow as a bamboo leg, because what they really mean is that they are unwilling to pay what the dealers will pay for the items in question. This is why some education in antiquing is necessary when you go out to buy. One does not have to be a mathematician to understand that the dealer is paying only what an item is worth, and that he will resell it at a profit to a collector. On the other hand, the average auction-goer doesn't want to pay what an item is worth, mainly because he is limited in funds when it comes to the ownership of fine pieces. Others simply do not know value, and therefore are in no position to be critical.

Advice has been passed to "Watch how the dealers bid, outbid them, and you will get a good buy." This may not always be a reliable rule, because at times the fraternity of dealers may protect their identities by various means. One is prearranged signals with an auctioneer on what signifies a bid. For example, a cigarette in the mouth means, "I'm bidding"; out of the mouth it means, "I'm done"; in the left hand, "a full raise of the bid asked"; and in the right hand, "half raise of the bid asked." Thus it is that many times no one knows who is bidding but the auctioneer. On the few occasions when I have been asked by an auction-goer to identify the person bidding against him, I have sold the item immediately to the other bidder. Then I have asked the questioner to repeat his question, as I didn't hear him clearly the first time. A good auctioneer will protect the identity of the bidders, so if you are going to watch dealers bid, you'll have to get a pair of glasses different from the ones most of us possess.

Another facet of dealer bidding has cropped up more and more in recent years. This is the establishment of what is known as a "ring." The dealers will band together and delegate only one person to bid on desired items. By not bidding against each other, they hope to hold the prices down. At the end of the auction the dealers group together to bid on the items the ring has bought. Any increase on the original price paid is put into a pool, which is split at the end of the day by all dealers concerned. Many times a dealer will make a good day's pay just by keeping his mouth shut.

Although I am an auctioneer and have had this done to me at auctions, I see nothing wrong with this procedure. It is perfectly legal, and just heightens the fact that it is growing more difficult to make money in the antique business. I find at auctions that not every dealer joins a ring like this, so bidding as a whole is satisfactory. But it offers no help to the novice who wants to watch the dealers bid in order to get free advice in this direction.

Early in the Spring of 1958, a short overall-clad man with a stumpy pipe between his teeth strolled into the auction barn one night. Busy as I was, I recognized him as George A. Martin, the "Yankee Auctioneer" from Maine. Recently, he had been pictured in *Life* Magazine in a series dealing with recreation along the coast of Maine, and his country auctions were pointed out as something tourists shouldn't miss. I had known about George, since he was a past president and secretary of the Maine Auctioneers Association and a prime mover in elevating the auction profession.

As is the custom, visiting auctioneers are always invited to take the stand. This he did, taking his hammer out of his pocket and bringing a small stone jug from which he nipped from time to time. These are his trademarks, along with a style of selling that is unique. When asked what is in his jug, he says it's just something that his doctor recommended. His pounding hammer will bring any sleepy crowd to life, and his quick patter and trigger mind have built him a tremendous following. He has been with me ever since. The contrast in our styles of selling offers a welcome change during a long auction. Barely over five feet tall, he is a dynamo in action, a clock that never runs down.

One night in the barn, a person brought in a dog to be given away; he was moving, and couldn't take the pup with him. George begged everyone, but to no avail. At this moment the dog, obviously upset by his predicament, chose to relieve himself in the middle of the floor. The crowd took off in gales of laughter, especially when George suggested the dog had proved he was healthy. Whereupon the dog did it again, and the crowd became uncontrollable. Just then a young lad came wandering in from the restaurant with hot dogs and drinks for himself and his girl. George, not one to let any opportunity pass by, grabbed the boy by the arm, thrust the dog's leash into his hand, and said, "You're the lucky one! You have just won the door prize for the night." It was fully five minutes before the auction could start again.

Another time, in Maine, the day broke cloudy and rainy. The auction crowd huddled on a rickety porch and George sold out of the doorway. As he turned to get more merchandise, he heard a noise and turned to see what it was. His crowd had disappeared. The frail porch had given way, dumping them into a small cellar below. Undaunted by this, his only comment to the crowd was: "After you've straightened yourselves out, I don't expect bargain-basement prices to be bid on the rest of this good merchandise."

One day in Ogunquit he was asked to sell a collection of Pop Art done by the natives of the artists' colony there. "My only problem," he told me afterward, "was that I didn't know when they were upside down or right side up." One woman asked him if he knew what he was doing. George retorted, "If I knew what I was doing, I wouldn't be here."

The manner in which he plays down his knowledge of what he is doing endears him to friends and strangers alike. His country-boy approach, often carried to the extreme of selling while barefoot, disarms everybody, and results in his measure of success as an auctioneer.

He tells the story of an auctioneer in Maine who was engaged in selling a parrot. The bidding was furious until finally a well-dressed woman from the city won out, and the parrot was sold to her. When she came up to pay the clerk, she remarked that she hadn't asked whether the parrot could talk. Whereupon the parrot piped up: "Who the heck do you think was bidding against you, lady?"

George likes to remind me of the night I was selling and he was feeding the merchandise. A comfortable wooden rocking chair came up and George worked on a man in the crowd to get him to bid more once he showed an interest in it. At last this two-dollar chair was sold to him for five dollars and fifty cents. After the auction I asked the man why he paid so much for it. He said he was very happy with it, because it matched one he and his wife had next to their fireplace at home. At that moment she appeared on the scene, and when she learned what he had done shouted at him: "Why, you damn fool, I brought that chair in here this afternoon to get rid of it, and now we have it back with a commission to pay!" Both George and I made ourselves scarce in a hurry.

One night while George was in action a heckler demanded to know who was bidding against him. Quick as a flash George told him that it was his Aunt Sophie, who was sitting up in the rafters, and proceeded to rattle on for more bids. The heckler, thinking he had George cornered, jumped up and loudly demanded to see this aunt. That was all George needed: he banged the hammer, shouting, "Sold to Aunt Sophie. Now, Aunt Sophie, will you please show yourself?"

Up rose a two-hundred-and-fifty-pound lumberjack, who, with a perfectly straight face, announced to the crowd, "I'm Aunt Sophie."

These are some of my favorite stories, but the auctions also have people with a heart. One night a four-year-old sweetheart of a blond girl darted from beside her mother in the front row as we brought up a beautiful doll. The family obviously had little money and the mother tried to console the child as others took up the bidding furiously. It finally sold for five dollars. I knew it was worth about two, and hardly handed it to the runner when the man who bought it piped up: "Give it to the girl down front, she needs it more than I do."

Not long ago a couple lost their small home and its contents in a fire. They had no insurance, but both were working, so they started buying household furnishings again. Most of the regulars knew of their disaster, and absolutely refused to bid against them on anything until they got on their feet again.

One time when I had purchased the contents of a store which had gone out of business, along with the antiques and furniture the man had were some Christmas toys and candy by the box. George Martin was selling, and when the candy came up to be disposed of, he noticed a family with many children near the front of the crowd. Sensing the kiddies would like a real treat which their parents could not afford, and knowing that prices had been good all during the auction, he put the candy up for bid.

Just as he thought—no bids came from that area. When the price of a dollar a box had been reached, he rejected all bids and proceeded to pass the candy out for nothing, just to make sure that this group got some without having their pride sacrificed by singling them out to get it free.

As the hands flew up everywhere, I caught on to what was going on. I glanced his way, and got the message as he said, "Well, your father told you to like gossip. Don't you?"

Uncle Frank Rowe was the only person for whom I sold merchandise without charging commission. He was of invaluable help to me, and also my closest friend. He lived on sixty-six dollars a month, a combination of an old-age pension check and his social security. He always said, "I live on seven cents a day, and could live on less if I cut out a few luxuries."

71

He made his living by using this small amount of money each month to buy and sell merchandise, so he could double or triple it to meet the higher cost of living. One day while riding toward Boston, we heard a newscast that told of a widow who had died leaving fifty thousand dollars to take care of her dog for the rest of its life. This was the only time in ten years I ever heard him lose his temper. The air was blue with real country expletives for quite awhile, until we pulled up in front of a restaurant for lunch.

I asked him, "Would you like to come in and have a steak with me, or would you rather be a dog and have a bone?"

He snapped back, "For fifty thousand dollars, I'd take the bone, and even bark for it, too."

One night he brought an old desk into the auction.

"For heaven's sake, Frank," I said to him, "where did you ever pick up this old piece of junk? What do you think I am, a miracle man to get someone even to bid on it?"

"Simmer down," he replied. "My nephew, Darby, sold this to me for a dollar. I'm bound to make something on it."

"Honestly," I said, "what do you think it will bring?"

He gave it a kick. "If it doesn't bring two dollars, I've got plans for this desk."

Just to help him out with the old wreck, we put it up at a good time, when the barn was full. Try as I might, I could get no more than a dollar bid on it—which was high at that. I couldn't resist needling Frank where he sat before me in the front row. "You said you had plans for this desk, Frank, if it didn't bring two dollars. Just what are they?"

His eyes lighted up and he shouted, "I'll show you!"

Striding over to the woodpile near by, he whipped out the axe and, to the consternation of the startled crowd, proceeded to smash the desk into a hundred pieces.

"There!" he said. "There's two dollars' worth of wood for your woodpile."

Unusual events like these always kept the barn full of people who were afraid they might miss something if they didn't come.

One day I was walking downstreet and met up with Frank and two of his cronies. "Let's go over to see Jud," he said. "He's laid up in bed."

Jud was one of Frank's older brothers. He was one of the last stagecoach drivers in New Hampshire, having driven the route from Union to Epsom for many years. He was barely bigger than a pint of peas, but he handled the four-horse hitch in a manner that would do justice to one of our Western movies.

So we drove over to Jud's house. Entering his room, we found him propped up in bed, thin, wiry, and sharp. Only two chairs were in the room, so Frank offered them to his two friends. After talking awhile, I noticed Frank fidgeting. Finally he blurted out, "Damn it, Jud, why don't you have enough chairs in your room so your company can set while they visit?"

Jud peered up through his eyebrows at him and snarled, "I've got plenty of chairs, I just got too damn much company."

Frank told me about the time he was courting a girl in Strafford. Early one evening they were walking out in a field behind the barn and they saw a cow and a bull rubbing noses.

"Gee," he said. "That sight makes me want to do the same thing."

"Go ahead," the girl replied; "it's your cow."

"I really liked her, though," said Frank. "Especially when we were drinking hard cider together. She was just like the moon, the fuller she got, the better she looked."

He taught me much about bidding at auctions.

"If you want something cheap, just let me do the bidding," he told me. "They all know I haven't a dime, so nobody will work too hard on me for more money."

We decided one day to use the hat signal. Just so long as my hat was on, it was his cue to bid; if I took it off, he was to stop. This system worked fine until a small bracket-foot maple chest came out. My eyes must have bugged out on this one, because it was a little treasure and, as Frank would say, "all curled in maple."

As the price sailed past two hundred dollars, people started to take notice that Frank was bidding.

"Mr. Rowe," said the auctioneer, "You realize you've just passed the two-hundred-dollar mark?"

"Yes," said Frank. "I've always wanted to buy one good thing before I die."

All this was happening while I knew he was checking to make sure my hat was still on. Just then the wind came up, a gust caught my hat, and away it went. Knowing I could never retrieve it in time to save the day, I stood helplessly as the next bid was thrown, and Frank said he was out.

We had a chance to examine the chest a little later and discovered that two of the drawers and one foot had been repaired. I felt a little better about it at the time, but today, despite these repairs, this chest would still be worth two or three times as much as it sold for then.

Bidding at an auction is not difficult if you take the time to inform yourself of the condition of the merchandise. At most good sales, there is an inspection of the items before the sale, and the auctioneers will tell you what they know about them. If an auctioneer will not tell you, I suggest that you start going to someone else's sales.

The members of our New Hampshire Auctioneers Association, as well as of other state associations across the country, are pledged to the Code of Ethics drawn up by the National Auctioneers Association. You will find these men and women members most helpful at all times, willing to tell you whether items are old or reproductions, and informing you if repairs have been done on them. It is up to an auctioneer to examine each piece before a sale to determine its authenticity and to be ready to answer questions about it.

74

The auctioneer who does not do this is failing to serve his subscriber and the public in a proper manner.

Quite often when an auctioneer does not know the quality or the value of the goods he is selling, you can make some very good buys. This is fine for the learned dealer or experienced buyer, and if you fall into either category you are much better off to attend such a sale and take advantage of the bargains you can get. But this is no place for the neophyte to be without guidance, for quite often he will spend too much money on the wrong items.

I watched a rather tricky situation once, where the auctioneer continually made fun of the items a particular dealer was buying. He kept calling them junk until the crowd laughed each time the man bid, and wouldn't bid on anything he started in on for fear lest it was junk, too. What a haul these two must have made at the end of the day, splitting up the profits on some really fine pieces that they got for next to nothing! This auctioneer is out of business today—as he should be, because the public will not be fooled for long.

Many people have difficulty locating auctions, so the New Hampshire Bureau of Markets started including listings of them in its weekly *Market Bulletin,* which is sent all over the country. This little paper costs two dollars a year, and is full of all sorts of information, mostly of a farming nature. All the New Hampshire auctions are listed each week, along with lists of farm items for sale; there is also an annual edition devoted to the listing of farm and other rural properties for sale. It is available by writing to the market bureau at Concord.

Perhaps your state has a similar paper. You can inquire of the secretary of your state auctioneers association, through the Secretary of State in your capital, and perhaps he can guide you to some source of information about auctions.

I must tell you of the first auction I attended, which was while I was in grade school. I walked home for lunch each day. One fine Spring day as I was returning to classes, I passed an auction and stopped a moment, completely fascinated by the auctioneer. He was affectionately known as Crying Sam Drew, and his trademark was a battered derby, which he would pull down over his ears from time to time in sheer exasperation when the bidding was not high enough. To emphasize his point he often took out a handkerchief and wiped away the tears that earned him his nickname. The crowd loved to see such an artist in action.

Soon after I began to watch, up came an old rocking chair; and try as he might, Sam couldn't get even fifty cents for it.

"Just think," he wept. "Some dear old grandmother sat on this porch in this lovely rocker, whiling away the December years of her life. There's love and devotion in this lovely old chair, and it can be yours for the mere price of fifty cents."

Out came the handkerchief to wipe his eyes, and he also honked into it a few times. The crowd ate it up.

Just then a voice came out of the crowd: "Sam, you sit in that just once so I can remember you in it, and I'll give you your fifty cents."

Eager to complete the sale, Sam thrust his two-hundred-pound frame into it just a bit too energetically, and it collapsed completely into a dozen pieces.

This was all I needed. That was the only day I ever skipped school, as he had me completely hooked for an afternoon which I think of to this day.

6

The
Art of
Buying

ONE MUST BE curious to be interested in antiques. Until he died in 1960 at the age of seventy-four, Frank Rowe still exhibited the curiosity of a newcomer to the business, and he had a talent for finding items hidden away in dark corners. As we passed many an old farmhouse on our junkets around the countryside he would say, "I'd give a dollar just to go up and look in that attic."

We certainly went through our share of attics, but in homes where we had been asked to come, or which belonged to up-country people we had known for years. However, an exception occurred one day as we were driving along after a summer storm and came on a large farmhouse from whose roof there rose what was either an unusual amount of steam, created by the heat of the quickly reappearing sun on the wet shingles, or was smoke.

"We'd best stop," said Frank; so up to the door we went, and the housewife answered his knock.

"I'm sorry to disturb you, Ma'am," he said, "but we were passing by and noticed what could be smoke coming from your roof, and wanted to let you know about it."

"Oh, dear," she said, and came out into the yard to look. The sight of her roof apparently panicked her a bit. "What am I going to do?" she asked Frank.

He hastened to reassure her, and gallantly offered our services to help her check under the roof for possible fire. Every corner of the attic was thoroughly examined and all was in order. When we left we had the owner's gratitude, plus chairs and a dropleaf table, and she had a windfall of cash for objects she'd not used in years.

Although Uncle Frank lived by the Golden Rule, he nevertheless got a kick out of "the biter bit" situations, or stories of the lengths determined people would go to in trying to outfox each other. One concerned a dealer who wanted to buy a set of four Windsor chairs that were stored in an attic in a nearby town. These were owned by an elderly widower, who had shown them to him once, but refused to consider selling them. Nor would he ever show them to him again, despite an extended campaign involving uncounted pitchers of cider which the old codger blandly emptied without relaxing his stand on the subject.

Finally, one evening the widower started talking about how he hadn't looked at another woman since the death of his wife, and there was a faintly detectable note of regret over missed opportunities for female companionship. The dealer sized this up as an Achilles heel, and proceeded to do something about it. The next day he approached an unattached lady of the town who made a career out of keeping house for a week here and a week there as opportunities came along. Briefing her on what he wanted and the rewards she might expect, he brought her with him on his next visit to the house with the Windsor chairs.

Out came the cider, and in came a gleam to the widower's eye as he watched his fair visitor become more at home with every glass. Then up came the subject of the chairs, and he answered, a shade absentmindedly, that they couldn't be seen. Whereupon the lady murmured that goodness! it was late—she really must be going; and over the vehement protests of her host she had risen to depart when the dealer made a suggestion.

"Give me another look at the chairs and a chance to buy them," he said, "and maybe I can persuade her to stay awhile."

The widower agreed in a hurry, and subsequently transactions took place to the mutual benefit of all.

I don't endorse such ingenuity on the part of professional dealers. And I don't recommend house-to-house or farm-to-farm buying for the novice. There are some crafty people living out in the back country, of whom Frank would say, "They can skin a cat alive without a knife."

I remember, vividly, the dear old girl who used to live atop Parker Mountain close by in Strafford. Regularly at my weekly auctions she would buy several boxfuls of china and glass. I knew she was not a dealer, and that she really did not have the money to put into collecting, so one day I asked her what she did with all her purchases.

"It's for the city slickers," she told me with a grin. "They come up to my place and I always answer the door in my worst dress; and when they ask to buy something, I let them in to show them Grandmother's old china cupboard. I don't say a word—just let 'em take advantage of an old lady living in the woods, and hope they'll want enough stuff so I can buy some more next week and fill up the cupboard again."

Not long ago another opportunist acquired an old mold for casting large iron roosters to top off weathervanes. A chance like this was too good to miss, so he had several dozen cast from his mold. Then he salted them down and later left them out behind his barn so they could weather and rust properly. After they had "aged" to his satisfaction he traveled throughout Maine and New Hampshire, peddling them discreetly, one at a time, to the best shops. Two of these phonies—which could never be detected by a novice, and perhaps by now not even by experts—decorate the roofs of two homes in one of the East's outstanding restorations.

Small items can be written off as the cost of experience, but when the newcomer reaches the point where the pieces he wants can be expected to cost a good deal of money, I urge him to go to reputable shops and auctioneers. For example: During the Depression unemployed craftsmen used available materials that cost little or nothing to make one-of-a-kind pieces in order to keep busy and bring in a little money on which to live. They would remove the drawers from Empire chests and build frames from old boards to reproduce bracket-foot or ball-and-claw-foot chests of the pre-Revolutionary period. Often the ball-and-claw feet would come from furniture made as late as the mid-19th century, and they would be mortised in so beautifully that you'd need to get up quite early in the morning to give yourself enough time to detect the imposture. Perhaps some of this work is still being done today, because many of the Empire chests with handmade, dovetailed and plank-bottomed drawers can be bought for as little as five dollars right now in our area, where the clumsy pieces are considered too big and awkward for our homes.

Sometimes I hear a beginner complain about the high prices asked in shops. These complaints can be groundless, as when the speaker just doesn't know very much about values and therefore doesn't recognize that the pieces are priced for what they are actually worth. Or the complaints can be valid—but sometimes the dealer is forced to put higher prices on his merchandise because he is weary of dealing with customers who don't feel that they've got their money's worth unless they beat down the price. If this is the game the customers like to play, they shouldn't be surprised if the dealer puts an artificial price on his goods so buyers who want to haggle can feel that they've bought something for a few dollars less than it was marked. Women are usually the ones who go in for dickering—and I often wonder how they would react if a dealer insisted that their husbands should "take something off" their fees for, say, filling a tooth or drawing up a contract. At any rate, people who dicker successfully for an antique shouldn't think that they're coming out ahead.

However, quite often a dealer in your area will give you a price consideration on his own hook if you buy several pieces at once. He would enjoy having you as a steady customer, and in addition will be glad to look for special items you want at only a few dollars' profit to himself, because you have not tried to beat down a fair price. Once any customer is pegged by the dealers, he will never lose his identity with them, and they will price to him accordingly.

Some buyers come armed with antique-pricing books. These guides are helpful, especially in the pricing of expensive articles; and the fact that many pieces are one of a kind is the reason for such a wide latitude in the prices quoted. Differences of characteristics and desirability also affect price, as do regional tastes and the economy of the area. Even when prices are not pinned down to the dollar, the handbooks give you some idea to start with. They are particularly valuable to collectors of bottles and pattern glass, because they assist in identification as well as pricing. Be sure to travel with the latest updated copies, since prices change so fast that you may be wasting time and money if you don't.

Many shopkeepers do not have prices on their merchandise, or, if they do, the price tags are unintelligible to the customer. These practices have led some people to believe that the dealers set prices depending on the size and make of car in which their visitors drive up to the door. Maybe there are dealers who operate this way. But usually shop owners furnish prices only on request for several reasons. One is that they want to avoid the nuisance of explaining their markups to people who sold them pieces from their homes and then come in several days later to see what the shop is charging for the items. Others say that they don't want to give the public free appraisals of antiques at home—especially when the public may fail to realize that the cost of overhead is included in the prices asked. Still others say that about ninety percent of their visitors are browsers who are really not interested in buying, and that this same percentage of their merchandise is bought by dealers anyway; regardless, the retail buyer is of minor concern to them, so why bother with price tags?

The fact that we all have a little bit of larceny in our hearts could account for the large number of successful flea markets today. These are nothing but a gathering spot for a lot of dealers—sometimes in an open field, sometimes indoors; I have seen them on the grounds of outdoor theaters, in old dance halls, in cow pastures. Generally these markets are run on weekends to attract tourists or people just looking for something to do.

Many of the dealers are genuine, running regular shops during the week, but here they are looking for different customers and the greater traffic such co-operative efforts attract. There are also many "attic dealers," people who choose to rent a space for disposing of an accumulation in their attics rather than selling outright to a dealer or consigning to an auction.

If you buy in a flea market, the chances are you will get very good buys if you get there early enough, before the regulars have skimmed off the cream, because most of the casual stall-renters price their items far below their actual worth. They regard the contents of their attics almost as junk, and price their goods to sell quickly so they won't have to cart it home again.

However, if the novice wants to sell his goods at a flea market, he is well advised to ask expert help in pricing: many times an item he regards as junk actually has good value.

By the way, a prospective visitor to such a market should not be put off by the "flea" in the name. The term was borrowed from the famous old market in Paris, where much of the merchandise was brought in from vermin-infested dwellings. But there seems to be no likelihood that this problem occurs at flea markets nowadays in this country, for in seventeen years of handling articles from all kinds of homes, I have yet to acquire fleas with the merchandise.

Even so, one should not be fussy about the place where one buys. I know of a tavern table that was bought for a quarter and passed through the hands of three dealers before it found its final resting place for sixteen hundred dollars. It was bought from the top of a truck on its way to a town dump. The original buyer followed the truck after noticing part of the table sticking up through the rubbish.

Regardless of where you buy, you should be prepared to make judgments on your own when the need arises, and here are a few pointers I have learned through experience which perhaps supplement what has been said in earlier chapters.

The best way to determine the authenticity of a piece of old furniture is to turn it upside down and look at the construction of legs and frame. This is where the mortising and pegging shows, while the age of the wood speaks for itself once you have learned to distinguish old from new. Ninety percent of repairs to furniture is done to legs and bases, as these are what suffer the most damage over the years.

Drawers should be taken out and checked, for these too get a lot of wear and often need work.

In furniture, the fewer boards used in the making of sides and top in a chest, or the top of a table, the better the piece. Those of single-board construction are more difficult to come by, so naturally their price would be higher.

It is amazing how small details are so important to worth. The thickness of a table top—the height of a leg—the uniformity of a turned design—the manner of dovetailing and mortising—the height of a foot—the design of a skirt—the authenticity of brasses and knobs in the proper period: these and many more little points help a great deal in determining value. It is not difficult to decide whether a piece is an antique, but it does take some learning to recognize one of good quality as compared with a lesser one, and to arrive at an estimate of their relative values.

As an example, take a fiddleback chair. A person will see one at an auction or in a shop that is just like another he had noticed elsewhere for such-and-such a price. But he should be leary of deciding value on the basis of "just like": I have seen more than fifteen types of so-called fiddlebacks, but some will sell for two dollars and some others, rightly, will go for as much as fifty. Condition, workmanship, materials, whether they are part of a set all contribute to the value. Differences in detail and quality that fairly shriek at the discerning antique-hunter can be overlooked by the casual eye.

Unless you are looking for an individual item to round out a set, buy sets if you can—but be prepared for an increase in the unit price. Just because one chair would sell for twenty dollars does not mean that six chairs should come to one hundred and twenty. The price could easily be two hundred dollars or more, for a premium must be paid for increased value bestowed by completeness.

And again I stress that pieces made in your own region or state should be highly important to you. Of course this suggestion does not preclude the collecting and enjoyment of objects made outside your area, but rather emphasizes the importance of local workmanship in that it reflects the heritage of your community and has its greatest worth there. An early tall clock made in Hingham, Massachusetts, will always have its greatest value in and around Hingham; and this rule applies generally to all forms of art. Without documentation of local craftsmanship, though, the pieces should bear lower prices.

I could go on citing tips like these, but I am not trying to write a complete guide to antiquing—at least in this book. I merely mention certain examples as a caution that, while there is nothing difficult about learning the fine points of antiques, everyone must do his homework if he plans to go out and buy by himself without seeking professional help.

Learning what is good, better, and best takes a little longer, but it can be done. And the working precepts are the same whether one is buying as a hobbyist or as a professional for resale.

Uncle Frank Rowe always kept telling me I was a poor buyer because "your eyes always bug out when you see a good piece." To control this deplorable tendency, he taught me to concentrate on the poorer pieces and include the better ones as part of a package.

He also taught me that it is better to do business with an informed person than with an uninformed one, as the latter has a greater sense of values. Many times we would be asked into a home where the pleasant lady of the house proceeded to tell us how "Grandmother was offered a hundred dollars for this chair five years ago, and how much will you give?"—this, while I was wondering if it was worth an offer of as much as ten dollars.

Sometimes these alleged offers by dealers are only an expression of wishful thinking. At other times they can reflect the pique of a disappointed buyer who consoles himself by "poisoning the wells." When he finds he can't get a piece, as he leaves he will say casually, "If you ever do get rid of it, don't take less than —— dollars for it." His comment is often interpreted as a spot appraisal, when actually the dealer is trying to defeat its purchase by anyone else. The solution to such impasses is for the seller as well as the buyer to know something of antiques and their worth.

I've already mentioned that a real talent for antiquing ran in Frank's family. His brother George had a national reputation as a dealer and Norman, George's son, also was prominent in the business.

When Frank's father brought his family, practically all on foot, to settle on a farm in Strafford, New Hampshire, after the Civil War, the first thing Mr. Rowe did was to sit down and count his financial assets. Other than a few sticks of furniture, he had one nickel, and a small rooster. Deciding that every farm should have a chicken to lay eggs for growing youngsters, he went to the next farm and offered to trade the rooster. His neighbor was friendly, but allowed as how a hen was worth more than a rooster; something more would have to be added to the trade. Then Mr. Rowe remembered his five cents. He offered it as the difference in exchange, and the deal was made. It was a good omen, for later he purchaseed a maple dropleaf table for a dollar, and on it his large family ate in shifts during the hard early days. This table is in our home today as one of our most prized possessions.

At the turn of the century George started traveling through the country as a tin peddler, and hired his young brother Frank to drive one of his big wagons loaded with needles, thread, cloth, dishes, brooms, and clanking pots and pans that announced their arrival long before they were seen. They started two routes up northward, which Frank and I followed many years later when we visited his old friends. Often the brothers would come to a farm where the housewife had no money and offered to trade household possessions for the Rowes' merchandise. These pieces would be taken back to town and sold to antique dealers, so George and Frank would make an extra profit on such transactions. His success in trading brought George the nickname of "Jockey."

On one occasion Jockey and Frank were traveling the country in the same tinware cart and they got into a minor argument. At the peak of it Jockey declared that Frank owed him five dollars, and he wanted to be paid right away. This Frank hotly denied, and asked for an explanation. Jockey told him that, years before, he had been up a tree picking apples when his father rushed out to him and asked if he had any money: their mother was about to give birth to another child, and he needed five dollars to pay the doctor.

"So," Jockey snarled, "I gave Father the five dollars. And he never paid me back. So I figure you owe it to me, otherwise you wouldn't be here!"

Frank told me later that he was the only person he knew of who ended up paying the doctor's fee for being delivered.

For a couple of years after my weekly auctions started, I would visit old Jockey. Although he was bedridden he was still the dean of traders, and everyone sought his advice and listened to his colorful yarns of the past. During one of these sessions Norman remarked that he surpassed his father in knowledge of antiques, and this raised Jock's fur: no son of his, he declared, could trim him at his own game. This triggered Norman to ask if he could try, with no hard feelings over the outcome. And the challenge was on.

Soon afterward Norman returned home in the evening with a large braided rug that had cost him only twenty dollars. Showing it to his father, he offered to sell it to him for thirty-five. Jock bought it, waiting until the money had changed hands before he stated that Norman didn't have any sense of values to sell him such a good rug for so little.

Then it was Norman's turn. He told his father that he should never have bought it at night because the threads were loose and it would soon fall apart; in short, it was a real dog. Jock kept on for weeks trying to unload it, but always in daylight when the customers would note its condition and refuse to buy. He acknowledged to Norman that he had been taken.

"I've shown it to the world," he mourned, "and nobody wants it." Yet still he refused to admit that his son had beaten him: he'd sell it all right—but after dark.

A few nights later one of Norman's friends spoke of wanting a decent living-room rug, and Norman talked him into buying the rug in question with the idea that the man's wife could make it as good as new with some sewing and stitching, but the purchase would have to be made that evening. Then he hurried back to his father, admitted that indeed he had sold the rug too cheaply at thirty-five dollars, and offered to buy it back. Jock crowed with delight and let him have it—for sixty.

The next day Norman showed him his friend's check for one hundred and twenty dollars for the rug. And with tears of chagrin in his eyes, old Jock finally admitted defeat.

It is no wonder, with such teachers, that my education in antiques came quickly. But Frank warned me that the business was full of pitfalls. "One day you eat turkey," he used to say, "and the next day you're eating feathers."

7

Background
for Antiquing

ONE OF THE FASCINATING THINGS about antiques in the United States is the variety of cultures from which they have stemmed. A quick look at the patterns of settlement indicates the major early influences. Aside from the artifacts that developed to become typically American, since 1620 our antiques have reflected the influence of—or were imported directly from—Britain, whose impact was felt over most of the Atlantic Seaboard before filtering westward; Spain, in parts of the South, all the Southwest, and California; France, markedly in and around Louisiana; the Netherlands, particularly in New York; and Germany, most notably in the Pennsylvania Dutch country. In addition, of course, are many influences that were less pronounced, or were felt later.

I think that trying to identify these ingredients of our cultural heritage, whether they are old or recent, is what I have enjoyed most. The search has taken me so far into many regions of the United States and into Canada, Mexico, the Caribbean, the British Isles and Europe. The following comments are a few highly personal reactions experienced during pilgrimages outside this country.

Despite the magnificent displays of artistic achievement

throughout Europe, we were attracted most by Mexico and the culture of its people. I guess many travelers are unprepared for what Mexico offers, even though their guidebooks cite attractions beyond bullfights, the cosmopolitan glitter of Mexico City, and the glamor of Acapulco. Not until we saw the emotionally overwhelming pyramids at, say, Teotihuacan, and the sacrificial altars near by, and learned that these are older and larger than Egyptian counterparts, did we begin to appreciate the grandeur of this nation's background.

Yet the Mexicans have a genius for living with and presenting the ancient and the modern side by side. Instances abound. On the walls of the central patio of the National Palace are Diego Rivera's powerful frescoes, representing Mexican history from the first Indian empires, through the Spanish Conquest and the revolutions of the 19th and into the 20th centuries, and the artist's projection of a Marxist future. This mural has been defaced many times since it was painted, yet each time the government has had it restored to its original condition, feeling that it is a work of art that must be preserved, regardless of its political statement. Sagging close by in the square is the National Cathedral, begun in 1573, and containing creations of unexpected artistic merit and almost staggering magnificence. For everyone who wishes to be surrounded by solid gold, and has never been invited inside Fort Knox, I suggest a visit to this cathedral—if only to see its decorations and religious ornaments and vessels. At the northeast corner of this oldest parish church in the Americas are relics believed to be part of a temple to the Aztec god of war.

And at night this square, the Zocalo, lighted by stark white floodlights, is perhaps the most beautiful architectural scene on the continent for feeling and simplicity of design. With virtually not a person or even a pigeon in sight after midnight, there was a quietness and compelling beauty in the massive yet fascinating buildings that surround it.

Tiffany Masterpiece in Mexico

The name of Louis Tiffany certainly is well known to collectors of North American glass, bronzes, and brass, yet his greatest single work is the scenic curtain on the stage of the Palace of Fine Arts in Mexico City. Costing $47,000 in 1911, it is said to comprise two million pieces of Tiffany glass fused together in order to spread across the huge stage.

The unself-conscious mixture of past and present continues throughout the Federal District, with mementoes of pre-Columbian times co-existing with ultramodern buildings of the University of Mexico and certain residential areas. Less than a day's drive away, the silver town of Taxco is an antique-lover's paradise, with much to be found from the colonial period. And alongside the gold, silver, brass, and wooden objects coming down from the era of the Conquistadores are workshops filled with silver and other metals of jet-age design.

I shall never forget my first view of the north coast of Ireland when I was serving in the Merchant Marine in World War II, with the cone-shaped hills rising in perfect symmetry from the meadows. I expected that artists would find much to paint in this area, but our tours years later through Irish galleries indicated that relatively little of this beauty had been recorded.

Vignettes of Edinburgh: Uncountable TV antennas atop centuries-old dwellings near Holyrood Castle are somewhat offset by the memory of Rosalie Chapel in the country outside the city. Begun as a transept for a cathedral that was never finished, it was later closed in; much of the glorious sculpture damaged by Oliver Cromwell's troops in the 17th century has been restored. The atmosphere of religious serenity is unmatched by any other church or chapel I have ever seen.

Back in the city, the antique dealers were busy buying the handsome brass post street lamps which were being replaced by modern electric ones. The old lamps, whose gas mantles stayed lighted day and night, provided a gracious and timeless note, and I felt that they should have been left standing, perhaps electrified if anything had to be done. Dealers bought each lamp for the equivalent of twenty dollars. They could have been sold for two hundred in the States, but the only feasible way to handle them would have been in shipments of several hundred at a time; and there was no possibility of amassing such a stockpile for export across the Atlantic.

Tea with our Scottish friends was an experience, just as it had been in Ireland. This is the time for family sterling or Sheffield to be brought out, and the assorted biscuits and pastries are served on Royal Crown Derby, Spode, Wedgwood, and occasionally odd pieces of Sapolian, Whieldon, or Turner. I think our hostesses delighted in casually using what would be museum pieces, especially when their treasures were recognized for what they were. It almost became routine to be served tea in early Staffordshire handleless cups. I was interested in the appearance of glass cup plates, and mentioned that I had thought that china ones were used more generally in Britain. I was informed that the glass ones were also made in the British Isles, and not all were made in the United States, as I had believed.

Without doubt the most elegant silver and brass items of the 18th century came from Britain. These are still used today —as they should be—and more and more Americans are collecting these items for everyday use.

I guess the English must get top marks for preserving their heritage of manmade beauty. Monuments, landmarks, old buildings are kept in good condition rather than being torn down and replaced by new, and at much less cost. The struggle for up-to-dateness for its own sake seems to have escaped England, and I think the people are much the richer for it. One of the tragedies in the United States has been the tearing down of historic sections of our cities and erecting in their stead acres of concrete and glass that look exactly like similar developments from coast to coast. I can not become reconciled to modernization which has caused the eradication of Scollay Square and parts of the Faneuil Hall market district in Boston, to cite a prime example.

Bette and I had visited the Spode distributor in Ottawa during our honeymoon trip into Canada many years earlier, and in England we saw the collection from the famed works in Stoke-on-Trent. The manager told us that Queen Elizabeth had purchased five different services for use at royal functions. The services of Spode that we own seemed rather pale alongside the royal examples. We saw dishes valued at $22,000 a dozen, and pieces of early work never seen in the United States. Our host was kind enough to give me a copy of a limited-edition history of Copeland-Spode that goes into details on their markings since the first days of manufacture in the mid-18th century. Without question, the English deserved their dominance of the world market for fine china.

In the Netherlands it was a thrill to walk the same cobblestones that had rattled the wooden shoes of Rembrandt Van Rijn. Surely Amsterdam can not be exceeded by any other European city for charm and beauty. We went along the picturesque canals and exquisitely kept old buildings to the Rijksmuseum, which houses not only a breath-taking collection of Rembrandts, but also hundreds of works by masters who are included in all standard art-history books. Only a fascinating stroll away was yet another museum filled with modern paintings ranging from incomparable Van Goghs to Picassos and Matisses, to name only a few. Everywhere the architecture lived up to its reputation—as did the diamond-cutters whom we visited and watched, entranced, while they worked.

Later we rode in one of Holland's swift and comfortable commuter trains to Delft, Rotterdam and The Hague. In Delft the wonderful bells in the tower of the great church near the marketplace seemed to begin marking the hour minutes ahead of time, and continued in a performance that caused even the natives to stop and listen. The many china shops are magnets for tourists. We learned that the finest Delft is labeled "Royal," with a crown imprint. There are many factories turning out the china and tiles, so naturally there are different grades of each; not all Delft ware can be considered fine.

In Rotterdam the outstanding thing to me was the dramatic rebuilding of the dock areas, which had been bombed to shreds during World War II. As the seat of government, and the home of a number of international commissions, The Hague offered almost a surfeit of lovely old buildings. Here we continued to sense the aura of close historic ties with the United States. We were reminded that in nearby Leyden, which has one of the world's great universities, many of the Pilgrims lived before they embarked in the *Mayflower* for the New World.

Somehow, Holland leaves its mark on a visitor. This is a place to which one must return, for the art, and the pottery and china, the brass, copper, and iron work are so individualistic that one wonders how a mere map-makers' boundary can separate cultures so completely from one country to the next. This is the home of truly great creators in all forms of art and manual expression. They have not been content to be just good: they all seem to want to be great.

We managed to arrive in Brussels when a huge department store was featuring a festival of foods from all over Europe. One entire floor of this building, even larger than Macy's in New York, was decked out in festive colors with displays from every nation on the continent. We were received with special warmth by the attendants at the Russian booth, who brought out their fanciest specialties for our approval. Along with their foods were displays that included many handmade brass items, in what we would consider antique motif at home, and which showed the influence of the French and Italian craftsmen whose contributions to Russia's art work are still to be noted. We hope we made as good an impression on the Russians as they did on us. We seemed to be the only American tourists present, as this was in January, and we must have received the concentrated goodwill that might otherwise have been spread over many more people from the States.

Paris is a wonderful city. It is too bad the people who come in contact with tourists don't share this quality, for we could not help but feel that we were being bilked at every turn. Nothing, however, could dim our appreciation of what the city had to offer culturally, and visiting the Louvre helped to compensate for annoyances inflicted by the populace outside. If I were an international thief and wanted to engineer one supreme *coup*, I would decide to make away with the Venus de Milo. She is the most thrilling work of sculpture I have ever seen, and I think the French are very clever in their manner of displaying her, for it is dramatic indeed to turn a corner and suddenly see her a long distance away with nothing to distract one's attention as one approaches.

Madrid, at the time of our visit, seemed to be a fine place for buying antiques. There was one section loaded with shops next to an almost continuous flea market along the streets. This was certainly the place for old glass, brass, and china. At a time when most American dealers were combing the British Isles for antiques, very few came to Madrid. I believe this must have been the place from which the British dealers replenished their shops; perhaps there were more problems in getting purchases shipped out of Spain than out of England, and such difficulties could have accounted for the situation.

Spanish and Portuguese shops were full of gold jewelry. The work showed the Moorish influence, which, I am sure, the artisans are trying to preserve. Many of the pieces we saw had an elegance not found even in France.

While driving through Portugal we were also struck by the many small villages having central town pumps or fountains that generally were set in plazas decorated with scenic multicolored tiles. The pottery we saw, all made by hand locally, looked just like what we fight over at auctions today in the United States. The tin and brass work all seemed to be hand-hammered, and I'm sure with a little aging could fool many an expert. Even the homespuns in one little market already looked a hundred years old. Much of the Portuguese landscape was like New England, with rolling hills and lots of trees and foliage, but everywhere were windmills and Roman ruins. In the excavations at Coimbra the mosaic floors were still as brilliant as they must have been twenty centuries ago, and the shapes of the windows in the few standing walls could start a trend in American home-building today. A quaint elderly man showed us around, and, although we could not speak each other's language, the shared appreciation for fine craftsmanship made our walk together from room to room most enjoyable.

Back again to this side of the Atlantic, we have found the Caribbean islands to have characters expressed by many nationalities. The scrubbed appearance of Dutch Curaçao is in contrast to the rather crumby look about Martinique and Trinidad. Haiti was desolate, with the exception of our visit to Katherine Dunham up in the hills near the port. I have worshiped this great dancer since the late 1930's, when I first saw her in Boston. She is art in motion. She obliged us with a dance done with one of the natives and her own musical group. Then she invited me to dance a chacha with her, and I rose to a wonderful occasion. Afterward she sat with us while we watched some voodoo dancers, and patiently explained the meaning of all their movements. Despite the island's aura of an iron dictatorship, Katherine Dunham's haven will remain in our memories as a favorite spot.

Masters of antiquing—"Uncle Frank" Rowe, right, and his nephew Norman. Below are auctioneers George A. Martin, the author, and Maurice Abbott, retired.

Both are pillowback Hitchcocks, but the one on the right is more valu-
able because of details in the feet, stretchers, and seat. The spool-front
bureau is one of many New England pine pieces still available.

The author showing his favorite piece of furniture, anywhere, to camera-man Lou Presti. A unique Dunlap chest-on-chest-on frame of the late 18th century, it is solid tiger maple, and has hound-tooth molding, carving in fishtail, inverted S, and shell-and-fan motifs, and heavy-kneed Queen Anne legs. It is in the Currier Gallery.

Demonstrating the heretical—and practical and beautiful—method of using flat satin varnish instead of the traditional penetrating oil as a finish. The varnish protects the patina and enhances the grain.

The Federal setting for Antiques, as described in Chapter 9. (The tall clock in the hall is not noteworthy, and the wing chair is a reproduction.)

Mrs. Alice Marvin at the Shelburne (Vt.) Museum explains some fine points of quilt-making during the filming of Antiques' first show in color. This program and others on location were made possible by an anonymous bequest to WENH-TV.

Discussing marine artifacts with Philip Chadwick Foster Smith of the Peabody Museum of Salem, Mass. This was one of a number of programs designed specially for the men in the coast-to-coast audience.

*With the Shelburne Museum's furniture-factory display rocker: from left,
Lou Presti, camera; Al Hotaling, director; Walt Maurer, lighting; the
author, and Gordon Mehlman, sound.*

The Caribbean and Canada

While in the Caribbean we took a side trip to visit college friends of Bette's in Caracas. I had expected much from this city, for in addition to being the capital of Venezuela it is the birthplace of Simon Bolivar, the deliverer of South America. However, architecturally it is sterile, and the extremely inflated cost of living calls attention to the poverty and resentment of the majority of the people. There was a good deal of old and very high-priced Spanish brass work in the shops I was brave and hardy enough to poke around in. The most desirable antiques I saw were the early pine bureaus, spool beds, Connecticut mantel clock, and the like, which our hosts had brought with them all the way from Vermont to furnish their apartment.

Over the years we have made many trips to see our neighbors in Canada, particularly in the Maritime Provinces, Quebec and Ontario. My first visit to Halifax was in 1943, when the Liberty ship on which I was serving put in to wait for a convoy to England. Little did I know that a year later I would be serving there in the Royal Canadian Engineers; or, for that matter, that I would marry a girl who has relatives in Nova Scotia and New Brunswick. The overall appearance of Halifax is old and interesting, with the Citadel dominating the scene and filled with intriguing relics from Nova Scotia's past. The antiques are mostly British, as there must have been little manufacturing in this area more than a century ago. Prices are rather high, but quality is good.

Throughout eastern Canada the visitor is struck by the mixture of French and British heritages, each of which has its own very definite character. Quebec City is outstanding for its Gallic charm—so much so that its Old Quarter was the motion-picture location of *13 rue Madeleine,* a James Cagney thriller about France in World War II. The museum at the Plains of Abraham, scene of the battle in 1759 in which Wolfe defeated Montcalm, is especially notable among the many places made famous in our schoolbooks.

To me, the most fascinating pieces of architecture in French Canada are the impressive churches that loom over even quite small communities. It is amazing how the individualism of each parish is reflected in the interior of its church. I remember particularly going with a friend to a six o'clock mass one Sunday morning in the little border town of Coaticook, Quebec. Behind the altar was a circular picture of the Virgin, nearly thirty feet in diameter, and made by gluing pieces of dyed eggshell on a linen backing. It was in this village, incidentally, that I came across two old brass fireplace fenders that are now in our home. These fenders are seldom obtainable in the States, but they turn up for sale occasionally in Canada. The duty was reasonable, as it is for many things one can't get too easily in the United States.

Ottawa, with its Parliament buildings, is the showplace for fine architecture inspired by English forms. It was in Ottawa on our honeymoon that Bette and I visited the Spode distributors. I discussed with them the varying prices of porcelain and fine chinas, wondering why there should be such a range for the services. In answer, the manager handed me a lovely plate with a pierced edge and asked what I thought it was worth. I hazarded a high guess, suggesting fifty dollars. The price was $1,400, and he proceeded to tell me why. Cutting the edge in its intricate design obliged the artisan who made it to work extremely quickly. Taking a hot clay "biscuit," he would have to cut it rapidly enough to go all around the plate before it hardened. If he did not finish while his knife could still cut the clay, he threw the plate away and started anew on another biscuit. Sometimes a couple of months might be required to turn out one such dish. Also, as a general rule, the greater number of colors in china increases its price, because each color must be glazed and fired separately. Since this means more separate operations, the price goes up.

Destructive Up-to-dateness

I receive many friendly messages from Canadians who are able to pick up *Antiques* on the educational television stations across our country. The Dominion has a colorful history and a vigorous culture, as Expo 67 has demonstrated to visitors from all over the world.

To sum up, I believe that Americans, particularly, should travel both in their own country and abroad, in order to observe and appreciate. Throughout the world, those individuals and communities who do all they can to preserve examples of their heritage deserve eternal credit.

The United States, from what I have seen, seems the least inclined to retain in everyday life as much as possible of its past. The whole communities of new apartment dwellings, the superhighways, the high-rise office buildings, the acres of suburban shopping centers are all necessary to space-age living, but many of them have helped to contribute to the demise of much that could have been saved if enough effort had been spent to do so. There is nothing either original or wrong in cleaning and repairing the fronts of, say, Federal period buildings, and restoring their interiors—and letting new roads and skyscrapers be located elsewhere. This attitude can be applied to any section of historic value, of course, regardless of what its date happens to be. The fine work done in this direction in Olde Town in Chicago, and in Pittsburgh, St. Louis, and Philadelphia is to be commended. Certainly these areas, and all others saved by persons active in historic preservations, have become just about the greatest attractions in the communities involved.

Which seems to prove that people all over the country really prefer progress that does not destroy. How about saving part of your community's heritage before it is too late?

8

On
Refinishing
and
Repairs

THIS IS THE AREA of "old wives' tales" in antiques. For some mysterious reason, to suggest a new method of refinishing an antique is almost heretical. Veer away from the technique of rottenstone, boiled linseed oil, and turpentine, and you are in hot water. But therein lies the tale of this chapter, so here goes . . .

A question most often asked concerns the necessity or desirability of refinishing. My answer is: "If the finish is the original finish and you can live with it, leave it on. But if the finish is not original, then refinishing is very much in order."

For instance, I have never seen a piece from the Queen Anne period to the present day that was harmed by refinishing properly. On the other hand, the early oak and pine pieces from the periods preceding 1720 can suffer a lot if they are not treated properly. If they have been painted since then, the paint must come off and their old unsophisticated look restored. This is work for an experienced refinisher and should not be attempted by a novice. If they have not been painted, but still have their old rustic look, nothing more than a good scrubbing with soap and water is necessary, followed by a heavy wax as a seal against moisture.

I think people usually want to refinish furniture only because the old surface is so battered that the piece would look out of place in a well-kept home. Many fine articles have survived so well because they were covered with layers of paint or varnish, which protected the wood from deterioration and small bumps and scratches. Almost any piece that is built in fine proportions and in good style will be made of quality woods. The desire to expose these woods and the grainings in them is the challenge that spurs most of us on to do a task that can be as easy or as difficult as one wishes to make it.

There is no mystery in refinishing. The procedure is to remove the finish without destroying the patina in the old wood. Even under layers of paint, wood will age; and this thin layer of aged wood is what gives an antique its charm. Brought to life again with a proper finish over it, this wood will glow, and the grain will accent the beauty of the piece.

The big problem is in what we use as a final finish. The removing of the paint or varnish can be done most easily with a good quality paint remover. I do not recommend the lye technique, only because it is a little hazardous: if used too much on a soft wood like pine, it can raise the grain and make sanding off the patina necessary in order to smooth the surface adequately again. Recently, commercial establishments have been set up to do this work for you, and if they use lye under proper conditions they will not harm the wood and can do a good job for you.

So far as the sanding goes, I use an abrasive block which wears itself away as it is used, so it never clogs as sandpaper does. It wears into carvings and moldings and makes it really easy to sand down a piece.

After using paint remover, a friend and I sanded down a six-graduated-drawer chest in only one and a half hours. A dropleaf table without too much carving in the legs can be done by one person in less than an hour. It is not difficult to remove the paint from a chair, sand it down with one of these blocks, and have the first coat of finish on within one hour. If you are using some other technique, you are doing it the hard way.

This same method is used whether it is hardwood or softwood. The block leaves the wood so smooth that even steel-wooling is not necessary.

Next, of course, comes the finish.

In the chapter giving tips on identification I told of the late Albert Gile of Rochester, the cabinetmaker whose artistry was praised by no less an authority than Israel Sack. Albert had worked on refinishing woods for years, and I stand by what he had to say. Namely:

If you put any oil or penetrating stain on wood which has been cleaned down, it is the worst thing you can do to it.

One of the great beauties of an antique is its patina, and this must be preserved no matter what we put on it. If an oil is used in refinishing, it will soak into the woods and remain there. True, it provides a beautiful finish; but as the years pass and the woods darken again with age, polishing, dust, or whatever, it may become necessary to clean them again so that the graining will show.

This time, though, it will be impossible to remove the finish without removing the wood, as it will be soaked with the oil or stain. And if the wood and patina go, the antique look goes —and you have helped in the destruction of it.

Albert contended that a surface finish should be one which does not penetrate the wood, and therefore can be removed at any time without harming it. Our ancestors used such finishes and this is why we can remove them so easily without damage. I'm sure that if you have tried to refinish a piece which had the old red-oak stain on it, you can understand what I mean, because this is the only early finish which penetrated the wood and is so difficult to remove today.

It is very simple to refinish with surface finishes that look just as well as any oil preparation. Our favorite is a very heavy liquid wax, which is applied directly to the wood and rubbed down. Several coats of this will give a dull sheen that is as fine as any you've ever seen. Any marking or scarring of the piece is removed instantly by rewaxing, with no harm to the wood. We certainly find this much more practical than fooling with finishes that soak in.

For those who insist on a finish that will resist marking, water-spotting, and such, Albert always used just a flat satin varnish. This again would give a fine dull sheen to the wood, and protect it, and was a finish that would come off instantly with remover at any time with no traces of it left in the wood. After the first coat, it should be steel-wooled to smooth it, and another coat given.

I have never used any more than two coats of satin varnish, because I have found this is all that is necessary. The finish rivals that produced by the finest oil treatments I have ever seen, yet without the hazards of oil.

Now, there are some who like to tone a wood with some coloring. The pines are too white, and some of the birches are too plain to take a clear finish, and tinting them in a soft maple tone is acceptable.

To do this, Albert would mix nothing more than burnt umber with the satin varnish and apply the mixture with a rag. The amount of umber used determines the depth of the color, so again you can make your own choice. Using an oil stain for this is fatal again, since the oil would soak into the wood. After the satin varnish and umber is applied, it should be steel-wooled down, and then nothing but a clear coat of satin varnish applied as the final coat. You will never be able to tell the result from one of the long, difficult, hand-rubbed oil finishes, yet the drudgery is taken out of the job, and the wood is preserved properly.

The technique is simple. Use nothing but the heavy liquid wax or flat satin varnish on the hardwoods. For pine and other light woods that need tinting, use the flat satin varnish tinted with the umber to create the tone you want. It is as simple as that.

If you still have your doubts about Albert Gile's methods, just visit many of our museums and restorations and see the pieces that have been finished with the oil technique many years ago. They are getting blacker by the year, and can never be brought back to lighter, cleaner tones without destroying the patina of the wood. The boiled-linseed-oil bit was the worst thing that could have happened to antique furniture refinishing. Albert guided many people away from it, to their eternal gratitude. Perhaps the missionary work in this book can serve as no more than a tribute to a man who was dedicated to the preservation of the old woods he loved so much.

Walter Calderwood is a noted attorney in nearby Dover. He is very active in the preservation of the Woodman Institute, the historical center for this community. A fine museum on early New Hampshire is maintained there, along with the old Damm Garrison, which is a log garrison building that withstood many Indian attacks in the 17th century. One day we discussed woods, and he came up with some facts that I pass along in case you don't know them.

We are in maple country and the figured maple woods are those most highly sought in our antiques. We call them by various names: striped, or tiger, maple; curly maple; birdseye maple, and even wavy maple. When one considers all these different grainings in the same kind of tree, he might wonder why they should be so different. Walter has advanced the theory that woodpeckers are responsible for the birdseye grain: as the tree grows, holes are pecked in it, and these heal over, leaving the small whorl marks in the wood.

The tiger or curly varieties can be caused by the following. First, disease of the wood could do it. Second, this could be its natural structure, and it just grows this way. Third, the soil content may have some effect on the structure. Fourth, trees that suffer a lot of compression in the wind from swaying back and forth would show signs of this in the grain created.

Walter says the old cabinetmakers always looked for maples that grew atop hills where the wind could get at them as these were the best grained. Also, evidence shows the grain to be the most pronounced near the outside of the tree, a fact which supports the compression theory, as the best veneers were taken from the outer layers of the log.

The native cabinetmakers used whatever woods were at hand and quite often mixed them. Many of our best country pieces can have a mixture of cherry, birch, and maple. A lot of mahogany was used too, as the merchant ships which traveled the world would take our goods to foreign lands and return with this lumber included with their cargoes. The woods from our native fruit trees were used extensively.

People are amazed at times to find several different woods in a simple item like a chair, but this mixture is easily explained. Most early chairs were painted, so a craftsman might use up odds and ends of lumber in his shop, knowing that the paint would cover the evidence of makeshift. This is why so few chairs are cleaned down to their natural look.

There is a misconception that wood must be solid to be good. Some people feel that because something is veneered, it has less value. This is very untrue. While the city cabinetmakers would use a lot of veneering and inlay to beautify pieces, the country craftsmen would beautify their pieces with combinations of fine-grained woods that were solid. To say that one is worth more than the other is academic.

More work was expended in doing veneering and inlay, and might often make a city piece command a higher price, but aesthetically country-made articles would be of comparable quality. Generally, though, you will find the highly decorated furniture bringing much higher prices than the solid, thus belying the notion that wood must be solid to be good.

Repairing an antique is something that should be left to an expert.

It has been said that up to ten percent of repairs to a furniture piece is acceptable and should not harm its value too much —although only if the repairs do not show and can not be noticed.

Legs and bases of furniture are the greatest casualties but here the repairs can be done so as to be unobtrusive. If old wood is available and the work is done properly, the repairs will never show.

So long as the drawer-fronts are good on a chest, the interiors of the drawers can be repaired without too much harm.

A table top can be replaced so long as the wood is old and in keeping with the original.

Old brasses are desirable, but the case reproductions which are available now do not detract from the value.

A dealer knows that it pays to be honest about repairs, so don't hesitate to ask him about them. If you do not ask if a piece has been repaired, quite possibly you will never know that it has. Actually, the buying of an item should be left to the discretion of the buyer and not the seller, and it is up to the purchaser to search out and identify all the points that he should consider before spending his money.

Here are some tips that may be of value.

Lots of old chairs like the Hitchcocks, thumb-backs, and

Windsors may turn up with a damaged base, seat or back. It is quite possible to find suitable parts from other broken chairs, and these replacements can be substituted in the damaged piece quite easily. We have one Windsor with a thumb-back set of legs beneath it, yet you would never know the difference, because they are of the same period and type of construction as the Windsor itself.

A good old pegged table-frame can be a good buy even though the top is beyond use or missing, as it is easy to find suitable old boards to provide a top. I saw a beautiful dropleaf piece made up of the tiger-maple top of an Empire table, combined with a Hepplewhite pegged frame beneath it. This made a table worth ten times the value of the Empire one. The fact of this combination did not bother the buyer—who was told of it—because the finished product was so fine.

However, the matching of different units must be kept in period, or they will clash.

So many Victorian mahogany and pine sets of furniture were made during the middle 19th century that it is not difficult to locate matching pieces whose parts will be interchangeable; being turned out by machine, they are very much alike in size and proportion. Many of the mahogany chests are nothing but pine with a mahogany veneer. I have seen a very effective chest made up of the mahogany frame of a round-cornered Victorian four-drawer chest, with pine drawers inserted to give a contrast of wood and color. Refinished in compatible tones, it turned out to be quite impressive.

Some people may be disturbed over the bumps and gouges that antique furniture can acquire through the years, yet part of their charm derives from this homely treatment. Also, they are very fine around children, since a few more nicks and dents don't seem to hurt them, whereas complete refinishing might be in order if such scars were inflicted on modern furniture.

To determine the ages of brass pulls, there is one tip that is almost infallible. Whether a knob or pull, if the threaded bolt section which goes through the drawer-front goes from the front to the inside of the drawer, and is held on by a rough, often almost round-cut brass nut, the chances are that it is very old. If the drawer pull is fastened to the drawer by means of a bolt inserted from *inside* the drawer, chances are it is a reproduction.

Look for alterations like leaves added to a lampstand, or a secretary back added to a slant-top desk, or a Windsor back on a chair with a scroll-front seat. Remakes done out of period, and some items that were never made in a particular fashion, require not too much experience to spot instantly.

We recognize the possibility of exceptions, so each piece must be examined. You might feel that a one-of-a-kind item would command a higher price because of its originality, but on the whole the pieces made in a standard accepted manner are safer for an investment.

Now, for the metals:

Brass can be cleaned with just a good scrub brush and detergent and water. If it is completely grimy, and green, perhaps you'll need the aid of a good polish; but apply it sparingly so as not to remove the patina from it. Shined-up old brass may have its place in some instances, but on the whole, that with a softly muted appearance is much more pleasing to the eye. I have seen old door knockers shined up, as well as andirons and the handles on fireplace tools. But old bowls, buckets, candlesticks, lamps, and the like, seem much better to me with their old patina.

Pewter should be scrubbed with only detergent and water. Do not shine it, as it never was shiny. If it needs real cleaning, a touch of silver polish will help take the grime off; but again, use it sparingly.

In the case of sterling silver, shine it all you want.

Do the same with the silver-plates. If the silverplating is worn so that the copper or brass underneath shines through, replating is very much in order, for here you are just restoring the original finish. This will not depreciate its value.

You might ask, why shine silver and not brass, when brass came shiny originally? It is just that the old-brass look is much warmer than that of the new, whereas silver does not look its best when dulled down with age.

Old copper should be treated in much the same way as brass, because determined polishing will take away its beautiful color.

You may feel that it is best to treat your antiques in a manner which pleases you, since you are the one who lives with them— so why not enjoy looking at them as you wish to see them?

I certainly do not quarrel with this feeling. After all, antiques are to be appreciated and I go along with the manner in which you wish to appreciate them. My suggestions above are made only in the interest of maintaining the appearance desired by most, and also of preserving the value of the items, which might otherwise decrease through improper cleaning or care.

You may say, "I have no intention of ever selling my antiques, so their condition at the time of sale does not interest me." If this were wholly accurate, just about all antique dealers would go out of business, because a good share of their transactions are with people who have to sell things from time to time for reasons they never anticipated.

Let's hope you never have to, but let's hope you get what they are worth when you do.

9

TV and
Antiques

M Y BROTHER JOE and his wife, Shirley, always entertain their
large circle of friends at a Twelfth Night party at their home
in Durham, the site of the University of New Hampshire, and
in 1963 Bette and I, as we always do, braved a snowstorm to
go.

One of the guests I was introduced to was Bridgett Paddock.
I discovered that she was from England originally, loved antiques, and was publicity director for Channel 11, WENH-TV
in Durham, the state's educational station. We had not chatted
long when she asked if I would like to audition a program
which was then being considered by the Eastern Educational
Network. The combination of my background in television
and my knowledge of antiques prompted her suggestion, she
said. Two weeks later I was before TV cameras again. With
seven lampstands, two of which were reproductions, I invited
imaginary viewers to select the new ones merely on the basis
of how I discussed them. This presentation must have intrigued
those in charge, because the plans for *Antiques* were drawn
right then and there.

I have always enjoyed challenges, and here was a real one: to make a program that would be informative as well as entertaining, to teach without the viewer's being aware he was being taught, and to create interest in, and desire for, collectible items that are still stuffed in attics and shops throughout the country. The answer, I felt, was to make it a primer on antiques, not an advanced seminar for the long-time collector; and moreover to let it cover the widest possible range of subjects, in order to reflect the innumerable facets of antiquing as an American pastime.

The first program was distributed to the twelve member stations of the EEN, which are all in metropolitan areas, plus some fringe ones that were permitted to carry it. As I write this, *Antiques* is scheduled to be shown during the 1967-68 season on seventy-five educational stations from coast to coast, via the Eastern and National networks and the Educational Television Service. These, along with many channels on cable systems, bring the program to some 2,500,000 viewers weekly, which is last year's figure based on volume of mail received. Thus is borne out our belief in the appeal of antiques regardless of where people live or what their backgrounds may be.

In the beginning, though, a number of antique dealers were disturbed at the thought of such a program, and expressed their fears lest the public become so well informed that it would be impossible for them to make good buys in homes any longer. There was also the feeling that an interest created in certain articles would bring about shortages, and hence drive prices so high that these items could no longer be bought at a profit.

Knowing that support from dealers and collectors was most important to the future of the program, since I expected to ask them to lend me articles to show from time to time, I countered with logic mustered from my own experience: it is always easier to do business with an informed person than with an uninformed one. Therefore I intended right from the start to drop occasional clues about relative values, but of course with-

119

out ever mentioning specific prices, as these could vary from locale to locale. Because neither age nor rarity alone can create value—there must be desirability as well—I felt that the program could do a lot to improve buying.

Actually, it has become routine for people to write in that they hadn't realized certain things in their attics might be of value; and, after the program called them to their owners' attention, the objects were dug out and sold to dealers and collectors who otherwise might never have seen them. Also, today shopkeepers tell me that items televised disappear from their shelves within a few days after each program. A case in point occurred after a show on stereoscope viewers. One man told me he had seen one in a shop on the day of the program. The next morning he hurried to the shop to buy it, only to find that he was the fifth person to come in for it within the first hour of business.

Responses like these have gladdened the dealers, and they welcome the program and advise their customers to watch it. When *Antiques* was first aired in Chicago, over WTTW-TV, posters calling attention to it were distributed to just about every antique shop in the city. The station had several thousand printed, ran out of them, and had to turn down requests for more.

The program was initiated under the direction of Ray Matheson, who was succeeded by Alton Hutaling when he later left the station to teach a course in government at the University. Together, Ray and I worked out the details of the set, and the plan of movement and display. The Federal period seemed the best atmosphere as a backdrop for the objects to be shown, so the corner of a rather informal drawing room was created by having a white fireplace, wallpaper in an early 19th-century pattern, and furnishings that include oriental rugs, a Queen Anne dropleaf table, Windsor, Chippendale and Hitchcock chairs, a Chippendale mirror, a primitive oil portrait, and a

rare coffin-case mantel clock made by Elnathan Taber of Rox-
bury, Massachusetts, around 1800.

I must stop a moment to tell about the Chippendale wing
chair. Not long after the program started, a fan who mentioned
that he was a Sears, Roebuck employee wrote in to ask me
where it would be most fruitful for him to look for a wingback
chair like the one I used. I told him it was simple: just look
in a 1961 Sears catalog, and order it.

The cameras might also be termed antiques. They are old,
requiring such intense, hot lighting that about five pounds
melt off during each program, much as if the filming were
being done in a sauna; so keeping the weight down is easy
from October to April, when the twenty-six new programs are
recorded.

For the early programs, antiques were borrowed from local
homes and museums. Then collectors and dealers were invited
to participate with items they would bring. Later our guests
were to come from several states away, sometimes arriving with
their cars loaded with cartons containing fragile and irreplace-
able objects. And in the Winter of 1967 an anonymous bequest
to WENH-TV for cultural purposes allowed us to make on-the-
spot programs at such treasure houses as the Currier Gallery in
Manchester, New Hampshire, and in Vermont at the Bennington Museum and the Shelburne Museum. It was at Shelburne
that our cameraman, Lou Presti, filmed our first color program, one on early quilts.

Trips away from the studio always seem to provide interesting experiences. Our first one was to WEDH in Hartford,
where we would film a program about Colonial and later silver
in America, with examples lent by Philip Hammerslough,
whose definitive books on the subject are rapidly becoming
collectors' items in their own right. The pieces we would use
were on permanent display at the Wadsworth Athenaeum, but
were to be removed for the program. And so they were: several

hundred thousand dollars' worth of breath-taking early American silver had gone inadvertently to the wrong studios.

This was retrieved safely, packed in picnic baskets and other assorted containers. Phil took the pieces out and handed them to me one by one. Rather overawed by silver which one may see in a museum but rarely ever can touch, I suggested that I wear gloves to do the program. He didn't think much of this idea, saying, "Good silver should be felt as well as seen." The casual manner in which he handled these treasures was proof that Phil appreciated them more for their beauty than for their monetary value.

Our visit to the Shelburne Museum was made during the coldest spell that section of Vermont had seen all Winter. Right next to Burlington on the shores of Lake Champlain, the area is in the path of northwest winds that sweep down from Canada, crossing first New York State and then miles of frozen lake. Our first program was done in an 18th-century farmhouse that had no heat, no storm windows, and no protection from a wind that ranged from ten below to a high reading of zero that day. Helped by two radiant gas heaters that affected only what they are pointed at and not the surrounding air, and the quartz lights that were used for illuminating the set, we did the show over a space of seven hours. Light-colored clothing is desirable for this type of filming, so I was dressed in a summer suit, not realizing the place was unheated. The icy air rushing in from one side and out the other provided my special challenge for that day. Bourbon was prescribed to restore our color and circulation before dinner.

Early airplanes were a subject proposed by a good friend, William H. Champlin, Jr., of Rochester. He is chairman of the New Hampshire Aeronautics Commission, owner of an airport in Rochester, and of course a dyed-in-the-wool plane buff. His enthusiasm resulted in our flying with him and full crew to the World War I Airdrome in Rhinebeck, New York.

More Alarums and Excursions

It was an early October day, and the splendor of New England in the Fall prevented any of us from sleeping along the way. The delicate blue of the Atlantic Ocean just off Portsmouth, the Great and Little bays in Newington, and the multitude of lakes and ponds in the area were framed in a blanket of color that no artist could paint. The reds, oranges, and russets were complemented by browns, golds, and the greens of the conifers in a panorama that extended as far as the eye could see. Flying southwestward, we soon saw Mount Monadnock in its fiery perfection, with Keene nestled deeply at one side. Then across the Connecticut River, and we cruised over the Berkshires until the elegant ribbon that is the Hudson River came into view with a tapestry of every hue and tone covering the distant mountains behind it. Reluctantly, we descended to the Rhinebeck airport and went by car to the old Airdrome.

A remarkable man named Cole Palen started this as a hobby, but it has since grown to be a mecca for those interested in heavier-than-air machines. On the last Sunday of every month during the good weather, spectacular flying shows involving old Fokkers, Spads, Nieuports, and the like, lure many visitors. A re-creation of the typical airdrome of the first War, it has a sod runway, and a curved landing strip which offers the unusual sight of a plane landing while coming around a corner. During our wait for Cole, we scouted the hangars to start making plans for filming. This is where we met the sheep.

These were two lovable rams which acted as watchdogs. Much to our dismay, we learned that as long as we stroked their horns, they were quite docile, but once any of us turned his back— alley-oop. Lou Presti and I were butted from pillar to post until we learned to play the game, because it was hopeless to try to beat a retreat. We were rescued by two of the pilots who arrived to welcome us. Our friends suggested that the best show could have been filmed right up to then, with Lou and me jumping from wheels to oil barrels to struts in our efforts to

123

escape from our woolly playmates.

Finally we started filming some of the old Curtiss and Thomas pushers, and witnessed the firing up of a 3-cylinder 1909 Blériot, of the identical type that first flew the English Channel. The motor responded beautifully for our camera, and as it barked and coughed the entire frame shook and the pilot had all he could do to keep it on the ground. The wing-spread of these old monsters was so great that it seemed as if a stiff wind would take them off the ground.

The peak of excitement came when Cole arrived and took off in his 1917 Nieuport. This French plane was very interesting to me, because the entire motor and propeller revolve on a shaft, rather than the prop and shaft revolving as in a conventional design. The balance tolerance of this arrangement is fantastic, and the fact that this aircraft was then almost fifty years old and still running fine, is a tribute to its makers. Another striking feature of the plane is that it has no throttle: it has two speeds—either stopped, or running full blast. It must have been quite a problem feeding gasoline to the rapidly rotating cylinders, much less figuring a way to control it. On some of the later 7-cylinder models, the firing arrangement was divided so it could run on either 7, 5, or 3 cylinders, and in this manner the speed could be controlled a bit.

Since Cole's was a "full blast" model, his attendants had to hold it by its wings as he stopped and restarted the motor to get it into position on the runway. Then they let go, and it jumped into the air like a duck taking off in flight. Lou followed in a modern plane with the sides removed for ease of filming, so he was held in only by his safety belt. He had been reminded by the pilot before he took off: "If you want some close-up shots of Cole in the cockpit, you won't need a telephoto lens— I'll rest my wingtips on his to steady you and the camera." These men are fearless, and are fantastically competent pilots, intrigued by what they can do with old machinery.

The Case of the Candid Curator

The final segment of this show was filmed the next day in Rochester, with later plane models in evidence, right up to a 1934 Waco which won a national prize for excellence in restoration. Dick Jackson of Somersworth piloted this 450-hp jackrabbit with me in it in a series of loops, turns, rolls and dives, while Lou was madly filming from another airplane. Accustomed only to the latest in airliners, I was unprepared for so many G forces, and the physical shock didn't wear off for a couple of days. About thirty seconds of this wild ride appeared on the program, but Lou kindly provided me with the floor cuttings as a memento.

Our trip to the Bennington Museum was made in the dead of Winter, at the invitation of its affable curator and director, Richard Carter Barret, who had traveled several times to our studios to do programs on Bennington pottery and art glass. To me, he is what every curator should be. He is extremely learned and well oriented, and is the foremost authority on Bennington ware, but he has not sacrificed any of his sense of humor or friendliness in performing his task. I think his love for antiques is superseded only by his love for people, and the projection of his personality into everything he does shows in this successful and most interesting museum.

On one of our programs, Dick Barret remarked that a type of glass now being collected was really "garbage," and the man who donated it to the museum thought so too, but they display it as an example of a collectible. Such frankness is refreshing, as one wonders if candor like this would be approved at every museum. He instituted a plan to display reproduction glass alongside the old pieces as an example of what to look for in determining the old from new. His revelation that the Rebecca-at-the-well pattern in Rockingham ware was made by thirty-four potteries but *never* in Bennington came as a shock to collectors who had attributed these pots to Bennington for years. I suspect he delights in shattering false illusions and old wives' tales about antiques as much as he enjoys the research, and he is performing a real service on both counts.

While planning our first program at Bennington we noticed, in all its nude glory, a life-size marble called "Nirvana" next to several fine furniture pieces. I suggested to our producer, Alton Hotaling, that it would make a change to open the program with a shot of me leaning casually on Nirvana as I made my introductory remarks. Furthermore, I told him, such daring and élan could very well earn him recognition as the Roger Vadim of TV producers. My suggestion fell on deaf ears, and we settled on a blockfront chest-on-chest for the opening shot. However, Lou Presti was fascinated by the discussion. He took light-meter readings on Nirvana before we began, and, as James Mitchell, the assistant curator, and I progressed from one piece of furniture to another, the camera gave the lady the recognition she so fully deserved.

I've had other ideas that weren't taken too seriously. At the end of the final program in a series on guns, why not let me take a derringer and feign suicide as the farewells were being said? Another show-stopper I suggested was that, after displaying some rare dishes, I should upset a tableful, smashing them on the floor. This would be followed by a remark that it was all junk anyway. The most colorful one would have been to conclude a bottle program by saying—"and this is my favorite bottle of all," taking out a fifth of a well-known brand of liquor and pouring myself a drink while the credits were being shown.

Guests for the programs have been selected on the recommendation of knowledgeable friends and sometimes by making arrangements with collectors who have written offering their collections and themselves. I enjoy doing programs with guests, because I feel that everyone has something a bit different to add to what most of us already know. Certainly I have learned many things from my guests.

My old days of radio interviewing have come in handy, as I

want to insure that the guest's ideas are projected, leaving myself in a position of seeming to be little more than a guide for the program. This is the way it should be. Practically all the time I know the answers to questions I ask, but I feel that viewers want me to anticipate what they want to know; therefore, while my queries sometimes may sound very academic or very basic, to the newcomer they are very important.

Occasionally a guest becomes a little upset when I won't let him handle and show his own pieces. Little does he realize the importance of camera positions and holding objects still. Most guests are a bit nervous, and they tend to clutch objects and move them around too much; and sometimes they tremble enough to keep the pieces in almost constant motion. For close-ups, an object must be pointed right at the camera, at the proper angle so light will not reflect improperly and "blind" the lens; and above all it must be held still, so the amplification of the picture is not blurred by any small motion. The few times I have relaxed this rule have resulted in what might almost appear as comedy on the screen, for I have tried to take hold of an item as a guest is waving it around. Some have been more concerned with my efforts to steady a piece in a proper position, than with what they were saying.

All the programs are done without scripts or prompting boards, as I am nearsighted and couldn't read them anyway. On some occasions, as when I do a program alone and have a multitude of facts and dates to remember, I will put masking tape with a few notes on the back of an item. This is quite rare, however, for a good memory is an absolute prerequisite in professional antiquing. I have seen a piece I auctioned over ten years ago, and have been able to tell the person exactly what he paid for it; so remembering a few dates, times and places comes quite easily as a rule. If I have had to do research on unfamiliar items for a program, I can read my notes just before going in front of the cameras and rattle the information off with no trouble during the show. An hour later, though, don't ask me to repeat everything I said, because all of it may not have been retained that quickly. Constant association with objects makes remembering about them quite easy. After all, have you ever seen an antique dealer bring a guidebook with him when he comes in to buy?

Our twenty-six shows are repeated from May through September by most stations to round out the year until a new series starts. The response has been good from all over the country, with the heaviest volume from San Francisco (Channel 9, KQED), and the next from famed Channel 2 in Boston (WGBH) and New York City (Channel 13, WNDT), in that order. Usually the letters are requesting the bibliographies I prepare in advance for each program, so most of the letters are handled right at the local stations. Many contain snapshots of pieces people want identified and priced; these are returned to them with a form letter stating that I can not do appraisals by mail based on the information given. Letters of special interest are forwarded to me, and I answer personally about twenty of them a week, which is just about all I can manage.

I have received only four uncomplimentary letters since the program began, and I suppose this is quite good when you balance them against those that have praised something about a show.

Once I did a program on stenciling, showing quite a few examples done on furniture and some on tin and iron. The Eastern Educational Network received an irate letter from a viewer who said I didn't know anything about it; that the technique that I described was nonexistent, and that there must be something else I could be doing besides pretending to know anything about the subject. In a letter to the president of the network I stated the case simply. The morning of the program I had gone north to Union, New Hampshire, to borrow the mentioned items from a man whose stenciling was sought after by buyers everywhere. His work was so good that I chose to ask to borrow his rather than someone else's. He spent an hour with me, telling the method he used in doing it and going into great detail. I described his procedure quite faithfully on the program.

I know there are areas of difference about this craft, so it is understandable there might be some criticism. For instance, there are some who feel stenciling is not done properly unless the craftsman is trained in the method prescribed by the Esther Stevens Brazier Guild. Esther Brazier probably did more to encourage a revival of interest in this art than anyone, and as a result of her teachings and writings, this Guild was formed, requiring a prescribed course of teaching and experience before an applicant is certified to join. In this respect, the Guild has performed a great service and its members must be accomplished craftsmen. Nevertheless there are some like my friend in Union who feel their methods are out-dated, too difficult, and too time-consuming, and in effect would tend to discourage Mrs. Average Housewife from ever getting interested in this fascinating craft. His method was simple and to the point, something anyone with a modicum of skill could do, and the results are as beautiful as any I have ever seen.

The program is designed to interest and teach, and to encourage viewers to take up rewarding pastimes. Therefore it seemed logical to present a less complicated way of stenciling. I never heard any more about this complaint.

Sometimes errors are made quite inadvertently. While doing a bottle program I referred to a glassworks in Covington, Connecticut, when it should have been Coventry. I knew this as well as my own name, yet when I watched it one night at home I was shocked to hear myself make the same mistake twice. If I had had any inkling that I had done it even once, we may have made some attempt to correct it, but I wasn't aware of it until it was too late. This must have given the bottle people quite a laugh. I hope most of them were a little charitable, and know that I didn't realize what I had said.

It was only natural that my being on TV would prompt people to want to meet me and invite me to speak. These visits with members of service clubs and charitable organizations, at historical societies and conventions have proved to be most rewarding because of the people Bette and I have met. The experiences are fun, too.

One we will never forget took place in 1966. In January my booking agent sent me notice of a speaking engagement at the Harvard Club on Commonwealth Avenue in Boston, for the evening of March 22. This was to be a black-tie affair, so I was obliged to order a new dinner suit as I hadn't had one on in years; and of course this meant a new gown, shoes, and the like for my wife. All preparations made, we arrived at the Club with some antiques for discussion and proceeded to have the attendants there take them in. Finding the secretary, I asked him where I would be speaking. He was rather surprised that I had come to speak on antiques, he said, because he had thought the program for the evening was on basketball, and showed me the bulletin board which listed the event.

"Perhaps, sir," he said, "you are to be at the Harvard Club in Cambridge."

Having left the engagement notice at home, I was at a loss as to what to do other than call my agent's office and hope someone was there who might know where we belonged. Luckily he was working late that night, so he dug out his file. There was a silence. Then he said: "I admire you for your punctuality, George. Your only problem is that you are there a year ahead of time—this engagement is for March 22, 1967!"

While speaking before the Exeter Historical Society, as is my custom I will discuss items brought in by members. One lady brought an oval piece of granite, perfectly hollowed out. Not really knowing what it was, I suggested that an auctioneer must use his imagination in describing items, and might expect this to be a mortar which Indians used for grinding their corn.

My description would fit an early Indian artifact, of course, but this piece happened to be the baptismal font from her old family church in Ireland, which had burned down.

At the same meeting, another lady told me she could get the picture part of the program well on Channel 2 in Boston but could get no sound. On the other hand, the sound came in well from Channel 11 in Durham, but the picture was poor. So she had had two television sets installed so she could watch *Antiques.*

It was at a meeting of the historical society in Falmouth, Massachusetts, that a member of the audience brought up a candlestick for my opinion. Recognizing it at once as a Tiffany, I turned it over for confirmation: it was a signed piece. She said she had the pair and wanted to know if they were worth anything. I told her the going price at the time and, as I saw the look of amazement come over her face, asked where she had acquired them. Rather shamefacedly she confessed she had been to her town dump that morning to dispose of some rubbish and found them thrown away on the ground there. Since I was coming to town that night, she decided to retrieve them and have me look at them. As Uncle Frank always said, "One person's trash can be another person's treasure"!

Arriving in New Orleans to speak to the Friends of the New Orleans Public Library, Bette picked up a newspaper at the airport. A columnist mentioned my coming and gave a great deal of space to an earthenware jar which had been found under the foundation of a building that had recently been razed. The name Manuel Piriz or Perez could be seen imprinted on the bottom. The owner planned to bring it to me the next night for identification. Since this was such a regional situation, I spent an hour the following morning at the library reading up on the past history of this fabulous city, looking into the arts and crafts especially. There was no mention of any pottery manufacturer in that area at all during the time when this jar must have been made, as the building was over a hundred years old. At least I tried, and told the owner so, the next night, with the suggestion that most likely it had been made in Spain or Mexico because of its appearance and quality, and the name of the maker.

On that same trip we went to Mobile, where we were treated to more of the famous Southern hospitality. I was invited to do a radio program about antiques during the noon hour. This was one of those talk shows where people phone in their questions about different things. I was so fascinated by the lovely soft voices of the Alabama belles that quite often I'd ask to have the question repeated, as I really didn't hear what they said the first time. During the hour the discussion turned to brass beds and their relative worth. I really wish the question hadn't been asked, because my answer shattered a few illusions, I know.

In the first place, all the brass beds I have ever seen are not brass, but rather brass-plated steel. The only parts that might be solid brass were the finials atop the bedposts; these might be pointed, ball-shaped, pineapple-shaped, or the like, and could be unscrewed and taken off the bed. When challenged, I pointed out the sure way to find out: use a magnet. If it stuck to the bedpost the material was steel, and if not, it could be brass. Since the South is loaded with "brass" beds, I can imagine what went on, because after my scheduled speech that night, "brass" beds seemed to be the main topic of conversation.

My trip to the Middle West was most interesting. Somehow, the Winter of '66-67 was a jinx for me. I spoke in Norway, Maine, and brought the biggest snowfall of the year with me. The night of an appearance in Boston before the Harvard Club, ten inches of snow fell. Four inches fell on my way to

Weston, Massachusetts; twelve inches during a visit to Portsmouth, and eleven inches at Kittery, Maine. After such a spate of bad weather, I remarked to one of my audiences that they were likely to read headlines saying, "Violent Storms Hit Midwest," as I was heading to Aurora, Illinois, the next day.

Sure enough, an inch of rain fell the day I was there, and the following day, after speaking at Green Bay, Wisconsin, my plane was forced down in Madison because of the tornadoes which hit the Chicago area. Pretty soon I won't be welcome anywhere.

People have asked how long the subject matter will hold out for *Antiques*. The subject is limitless, and so are the possibilities; in five years, we have barely scratched the surface.

My only regret is that I can not write personally to all the people I feel have become my friends through the program. Some day, perhaps when the boys are all in college, Bette and I can visit all the kind people who have written to invite us to be their guests and talk about old and beautiful and interesting objects from the past.

Until then, I say: "Happy antiquing!"

Some
Reference Books

THE FOLLOWING are a few titles selected from the bibliographies prepared for each *Antiques* program. Most of the books are available at your bookstore; out-of-print titles are generally to be found in your public library, and those with limited distribution are obtainable from the person or institution publishing them.

"WHAT IS IT?"

Antique Collector's Guide to New England by Polly Webster; New York, Grosset & Dunlap.

Complete Book of Small Antiques Collecting by Katharine McClintock; New York, Coward-McCann.

Hitting the Antiques Trail by Ann Kilborn Cole; New York, David McKay.

Living with Antiques by Antiques Magazine and Helen Winchester, ed.; New York, Dutton.

AMERICAN GLASS

American Glass by Helen and George S. McKearin; New York, Crown.

American Pressed Glass & Figure Bottles by Albert Christian Revi; New York, Thomas Nelson & Sons.

"Corning Glass Center" (booklet); Corning, N. Y.

Early American Pattern Glass Book II by Alice Metz; published by the author, 2004 West 102nd St., Chicago, Ill.

Early American Pressed Glass by Ruth Webb Lee; published by the author, Framingham Center, Mass.

The Identification of American Art Glass by Richard Carter Barret; published by the author, Bennington, Vt.

POTTERY AND PORCELAIN

Bennington Pottery and Porcelain by Richard Carter Barret; New York, Crown.

Chinese Export Porcelain for the American Trade by Jean McClure Mudge; Newark, Del., University of Delaware Press.

Early New England Potters and Their Wares by Lura W. Watkins; Cambridge, Harvard University Press.

Handbook of Old Pottery and Porcelain Marks by C. Jordan Thorn; New York, Tudor.

Handbook of Pottery and Porcelain Marks by J. P. Cushion and W. B. Honey; New York, Pitman.

How to Identify Bennington Pottery by Richard Carter Barret; Brattleboro, Vt., Stephen Greene Press.

FURNITURE AND REFINISHING

American Furniture of the Federal Period by Charles F. Montgomery; New York, Viking.

American Furniture: Queen Anne and Chippendale Periods by Joseph Downs; New York, Macmillan.

Classical America 1815-1845 (Loan Exhibition Catalogue); Newark (N. J.) Museum.

Complete Book of Furniture-Repair and Refinishing by Ralph Parsons Kunney; New York, Scribners.

Field Guide to Early American Furniture by Thomas H. Ormsbee; Boston, Little, Brown.

Fine Points of Furniture: Early American by Albert Sack.

Furniture Refinishing at Home by Nina Glenn Joyner; Philadelphia, Chilton.

Furniture Treasury by Wallace Nutting; 2 vols.; New York, Macmillan.

CLOCKS

American Clocks and Clockmakers by Carl W. Drepperd; Garden City, N. Y., Doubleday.

Book of American Clocks by Brooks Palmer; New York, Macmillan.

The Clock Book by Wallace Nutting; Framingham, Mass., Old America.

MISCELLANEOUS

American Pewter by J. B. Kerfoot; New York, Crown.

Antique Airplane Association Publications; Fremont, Iowa.

The Book of the American Bell Association by the American Bell Association; Tarentum, Pa.

Collecting Antique Jewelry by Mona Curran; New York, Emerson.

The Collecting of Guns edited by James E. Severn; Harrisburg, Pa., Stackpole.

Dolls: A New Guide for Collectors by Clara E. Fawcett; Newton Centre, Mass., Charles T. Branford.

Handbook of Old American Toys by Louis H. Hertz; Wethersfield, Conn., Mark Haber & Co.

The New-York Historical Society's Dictionary of Artists in America 1564-1860 by George C. Groce and David H. Wallace; New Haven, Yale University Press.

The Standard Book of Quilt Making and Collecting by Margaret Ickis; New York, Dover Publications.

Stereo Views by W. C. Darrah, RFD #1, Gettysburg, Pa.